PHYSICAL EDUCATION

The Essential Toolkit
for Primary School Teachers

Written by
GERALD GRIGGS

First Published
April 07 in Great Britain by

PUBLISHING

A CIP record for this work is available from the British Library

ISBN-10: 1-905637-13-6
ISBN-13: 978-1-905637-13-3

Typeset by Educational Printing Services Limited

Educational Printing Services Limited

site: www.eprint.co.uk

ACKNOWLEDGEMENTS

This book represents something of a journey of learning and development, so thank you to all of you who have made the journey so interesting, for investing your time and giving encouragement along the way.

Specifically I would like to thank Vicky Harrhy, Pat Grant, David Murrie, Kevin Tomlin, Jackie Pawsey, Sue Cooke, Carol Lukins, John Mitcheson, Alan Lindsay, Terry Harris, Lincoln Allison, Terry Monnington, Andrew Parker, Yahya Al-Nakeeb, Lorayne Woodfield, Christine Davies, Kim Wheeler, Ian Pickering, Liz Taplin, Sheila Wigmore and Linda Wilkinson. In different ways you have all contributed in enabling me to get this far and for that I am truly grateful.

Lastly but by no means least, I would like to thank my wife Bernadette for all her love and support and for always encouraging me to follow my dreams.

CONTENTS

INTRODUCTION

Who is this book for?

This book is aimed at all those responsible for delivering Primary Physical Education (PE), principally classroom teachers, teacher trainers and ITT students. The rationale for such a resource lies in the fact that the current training afforded to trainees in PE is insufficient nationally. With the expansion of teacher training being delivered increasingly by one year PGCE courses, currently PE can account for as little as six hours of the total programme. Given that the National Curriculum for PE is comprised of Games, Dance, Gymnastics, Athletics, Outdoor and Adventurous Activities and Swimming, it is no wonder that OFSTED have started to raise concerns of how current training needs are meeting the breadth required by law.

Why is this book needed now?

With PE a compulsory element of the National Curriculum in England and Wales and soon, with the further development of the PE, School Sport and Club Links Strategy (PESSCL) and the Extended School initiative (8-6 opening), schools will have to guarantee at least two hours curriculum time per week for PE and another two hours extra curricular provision. It is feared that without the depth of training, primary practitioners will be unable to deliver the breadth of curriculum required to the appropriate standard. What this book hopes to provide is a resource that will support Primary practitioners by offering advice and guidance, as well as providing a resource that can be 'dipped into' when looking for an effective, practical way to teach an activity in any of the six areas of the National Curriculum for Physical Education (NCPE).

Why is this book easy to use?

The book is essentially in two parts. Part one addresses key areas to consider when teaching Physical Education, such as planning and differentiation but embeds them within a user friendly and practical structure of points to consider - before the lesson, at the start of the lesson, during the main part of the lesson, at the end of the lesson and after the lesson.

The second part specifically addresses the teaching of the NCPE and provides well tried and trusted illustrated lesson ideas for each of the main areas of the NCPE, namely Games, Dance, Gymnastics, Athletics, Outdoor and Adventurous Activities and Swimming.

Overall, it is hoped that the information contained within this book will support and provide invaluable advice for all that use it and will not only empower the practitioner to deliver effective Physical Education but will enthuse and inspire the next generation of young people to actively participate and reach their full potential.

PART ONE

How to teach
Primary Physical Education

BEFORE THE LESSON

DON'T 'TURN CHILDREN OFF' PE

It is fair to say that many practitioners can identify areas of the National Curriculum that they feel less than confident teaching. For some, the thought of having to teach Physical Education will come at the bottom of their list. The reasons for such perceptions can be many and varied ranging from feeling unsure about subject knowledge, to having bad experiences of PE whilst at school. Regardless of what has caused such an opinion, the important factor is that as teachers we do not transmit the same values on to the children we teach!

If for instance we teach in a less than enthusiastic manner, with closed body language and fail to change into appropriate clothing (just putting trainers on instead of shoes is not enough!), then this sends a clear message of what our expectations are of this lesson. Be as enthusiastic as possible and lead by example, even if you believe you can't 'turn pupils on to PE', at the very least 'don't turn them off it!'

FOLLOW SCHOOL POLICY

Though the mark of a high quality teacher is always having high expectations of their class it is also important to remember to know and follow school policies, procedures and routines before implementing PE sessions. For instance, 'Has the ground been checked to see if it's too wet or too hard?' 'Do you know what to do if a child has an accident when teaching on the far field?' 'Is the hall free today? Was the school timetable checked to see that there were no clashes?'

Though some of these issues may seem mundane, should anything go wrong, for example, a child seriously hurts themselves, a key question that may be asked is 'Was school policy followed?'

JEWELLERY

Jewellery policies vary considerably from school to school and from one Local Authority to another, so always check what the appropriate line is. Generally, children should remove all jewellery before starting a PE lesson and in cases where this may prove problematic, such as a child with newly pierced ears or where a child cannot remove a religious adornment, the item can often be secured safely with tape or plasters. Having a chat with parents or guardians at an early stage will usually clarify any further complications.

SAFETY

Again, policies on safety procedures such as carrying out risk assessments vary considerably from school to school and from one Local Authority to another, so always check what the appropriate line is. Largely, the official documentation is handled by a senior member of staff, so is unlikely to be a huge concern for those new to the profession. However, when taking children away from the school premises, it is important to find out who is responsible for such matters, so that all the relevant details can be compiled e.g. names of children, contact numbers etc.

On a day to day basis, concern should be given to three main areas – the people involved (teachers, AOTTs, children), the activity itself and the context in which it occurs, including the equipment and the playing area. In all situations 'common sense' should be applied and if there is any doubt, it is always best to err on caution. Specifically, most Local Authorities and schools use a document entitled 'Safe Practice in PE and Sport' (see Useful References) for detailed guidance on a day to day basis and this should be consulted if clarification of a particular issue is required.

CONSIDER PRIOR LEARNING

Taking into consideration what prior learning has taken place is vital for two reasons. Firstly, effective teaching and learning is more likely to take place if the lesson builds upon experiences already gained. It is unlikely, for instance, that a child would be able to execute a dive forward roll, if they had yet to experience a basic forward roll. This leads on to the now obvious second point which relates to safety. It is not safe for children to engage in higher order skills referred to above without the correct foundations. This also applies when introducing new equipment such as hockey sticks. It is far too dangerous to allow children to play a game or engage in any form of contact before they learn how to control a stick properly.

Before any kind of planning takes place, try and consult with former teachers and/or the PE subject leader to ascertain what the children have already covered. One should be wary of asking the children what they have done or can do, as the answers may not be as accurate as required. Try asking a group of young children who can swim and see how many hands go up. Match this with how many children can actually swim after seeing them in the water and be alarmed at the difference!

CONSULT EXISTING PLANNING

In order to maintain the planned progression of the childrens' Physical Education throughout the school, endeavour to follow the indicated scheme or unit of work. For many non-specialists this is a welcome crutch because detailed units of work tell the teacher exactly what to do for each lesson. Most Primary schools employ the QCA Schemes of Work at least for structural purposes and then devise appropriate activities to best meet the specified objectives (see part 2). Such units are also useful to keep in focus what is most important for the age and ability of the children, rather than impose preconceived ideas about what should be taught.

CONSULT PREVIOUS EVALUATIONS

The very best planning draws upon reflected experiences, so if evaluations exist of previous lessons or units, use them (see later pages on lesson evaluations). The best teachers don't make the same mistake twice!

SEEK ADVICE FROM THE PE SUBJECT LEADER

If in doubt about any matters concerning Physical Education in school, always consult with the PE subject leader. Even if they are not able to help directly, they are usually best placed to indicate where to go next.

DON'T FORGET THE FOUR STRANDS!

Though the National Curriculum is divided into six activity areas, just providing activities for those areas is not enough. Thought must also be given to the four strands of knowledge, skills and understanding identified in the programmes of study, namely:

- Acquiring and developing skills

- Selecting and applying skills, tactics and compositional ideas

- Knowledge and understanding of fitness and health

- Evaluating and improving

All these strands are of equal importance, so attention must be given to them during the planning stage. Traditionally what occurs during PE lessons is an over emphasis on Acquiring and Developing skills, so endeavour to facilitate opportunities that allow children to experience a full range of learning.

PLAN FOR SIMPLE TRANSITIONS

Well planned lessons with engaging activities can end up being ineffective if transitions between different parts of the lesson are not well managed. Nowhere is this more evident than when asking children to get into groups. You will need to consider how you can effectively move from one activity to another without creating undue fuss or delay.

RESOURCES

The success of a lesson can depend on many things, not least the equipment that is chosen. For example, some balls bounce higher than others, some do not roll well on grass and some blow away on a windy day. The task is to choose the right equipment that will most effectively assist in the learning that is taking place. This can sometimes be trial and error but most ideas can be worked out in advance, especially if a little bit of rehearsal has taken place already.

IDENTIFY PUPILS FOR ASSESSMENT

Sometimes the idea of assessing in Physical Education seems daunting, not least because there are a class full of children moving about whilst you are trying to do it. In order to sharpen the focus of this process, identify pupils who are to be the focus of your attention. It is important also not to over stretch yourself - a maximum of six pupils would be a challenge for an experienced teacher.

The selected pupils can then become the focus of key questions in the introduction and more likely the plenary. Such key questions should relate to both the objectives and the outcomes of the session and provide a window into how well the pupils understand. The responses will provide even more information not only for records but more importantly, where the pupils need to go next.

DIFFERENTIATION

In order that children make the maximum amount of progress, consideration must be given to matching the right activity to the right child. Differentiation is a challenge at the best of times in a mixed ability class and to achieve it consistently is the mark of an excellent teacher. In Physical Education, it is an area that is often neglected but it is just as vital in this area of the curriculum as it is in any other.

If starting from scratch in this area, look at the expectations for each of the QCA units of work. These provide statements for three different levels and are organised into:

- most children will be able to

- some children will not have made so much progress

- some children will have progressed further.

Once a feel is gained as to where the children are going, appropriate activities can then be devised. Care must be taken, however, not to impose unachievable goals upon pupils, so close consideration must be paid to all assessments made and all work completed so far.

As our understanding develops, our differentiation skills should become more sophisticated. Catering for the broadest range of pupils may well require conversations with those in the school responsible for Special Educational Needs as well as Gifted and Talented pupils. In such instances, ascertain what steps the pupils have already taken and are likely to take next (ask former/next teacher, PE subject leader, school units of work). This should provide a clearer picture as to what might need to be reinforced regarding the three different levels indicated above.

Also, it must be remembered that differentiating by outcome is often not the most appropriate way to maximise pupil progress (though it's clearly the easiest). Consideration should also be given to differentiating by varying the tasks set, the resources provided and the support given to optimise learning.

50% ACTIVITY

Though there is no stipulation as to how much activity children should actually engage in, given the fact that the lesson is dealing with education in a physical form, it seems natural to try and aim high. A figure of at least 50% may not seem much but once all the different components of the lesson are taken into account, such as transitions, moving around equipment and direct teaching, a teacher will do well to achieve this.

TEACHING APPROACHES

As a key component of teaching is to communicate information effectively it is important to give consideration into the different ways this can be facilitated. The following points are no way a comprehensive overview of the topic but offer four distinct ways in which a teacher might approach a lesson or part of a lesson.

INSTRUCTOR

Those that use an 'instructor' teaching style tend to focus on content/subject knowledge. This style is generally teacher-centred, where the teacher is responsible for providing and controlling the flow of the content and the child is expected to receive it.

DEMONSTRATOR

Teachers who have a demonstrator teaching style tend to run teacher-centred classes with an emphasis on demonstration and modelling. This type of teacher acts as a role model by demonstrating skills and processes and then as a guide in helping children develop and apply these skills and knowledge.

FACILITATOR

Teachers who have a facilitator model teaching style tend to focus on activities. This teaching style emphasises child-centred learning, with much more responsibility placed on the children to take the initiative for meeting the demands of various learning tasks.

DELEGATOR

Teachers who have a delegator teaching style tend to place much control and responsibility for learning on individuals or groups of children. Adopting this role will often give children a choice in designing and implementing their own learning, with the teacher acting in a consultative role.

Each mode of delivery has it strengths and weaknesses and will feel more or less comfortable in different situations. It is therefore a good idea to try them all out from time to time, to see which works best. It will also open up the idea that the mode of delivery does not have to be conducted in the same way every time.

REHEARSE

If faced with an activity that seems very unfamiliar e.g. dribbling a football, holding a hockey stick or demonstrating a dance routine, then the only thing to do is to practise. Increased familiarity with an object will show a quick return in improving both confidence and ability. Similarly rehearsing specific movements especially with the use of a mirror will show similar improvements. Where this will make the biggest impact is during demonstrations to children, as the quality that is required can be clearly demonstrated. Though it is also possible to ask other pupils to demonstrate instead (and is advisable if you really can't match the quality required), it does not send such a powerful message. This is most obvious when needing to break down additional barriers such as gender associated activities. For example, nothing opens up the idea to boys that they can dance more than a male teacher showing them that they can. The same is also true when female teachers demonstrate their football skills.

USE SPECIFIC VOCABULARY

Just as it is important to equip children with appropriate vocabulary when engaging in other areas of the curriculum like numeracy and literacy, it is important to teach and use the most suitable words and phrases during PE. In most cases, suitable vocabulary can be located on relevant lists e.g. QCA schemes of work for PE and should be displayed and used whenever appropriate (see later pages on activity specific vocabulary).

USE EQUITABLE VOCABULARY

Some vocabulary that is used in sport has become so ingrained in our culture that we are not always aware of the connotations that could be attached to it. An obvious example is when we talk of employing the defensive strategy of 'man to man' marking. Though some may say that to use 'person to person' or 'one to one' instead is an example of political correctness gone mad, it illustrates at least the point about the importance of questioning even the small things that we do.

PREPARE AREA

Whether the area to be used is appropriate or not is largely a matter of health and safety. That said common sense should still be applied to all situations. If the school is an open site, it may be accessed by members of the public (not always legally) after school hours. PE lessons first thing in the morning can often turn up a whole host of interesting finds! If the school has a sand pit, this should also be checked thoroughly. Such places have been known to attract broken glass, needles and animal excrement. Also, if PE is to take place after lunch, the floor may need to be checked for stray bits of food.

PLANNING

Planning lessons is not an exact science but what can help in the construction of a high quality lesson is the production of an effective plan to work from, which enables us to identify the structure of the session such as the sequence of events and the teaching points we want to communicate.

During training or inspection, the completion of lesson plans can often seem an onerous task and this is often because they are produced as a paper work exercise, rather than a document that is used to support the teaching of the session.

The format that is most effective is arguable and varies considerably from school to school. What is important is that a format can be used to enable us to plan effectively and if it does not work, should be modified. On the following pages are blank examples that can be used for such a task. Sheet one identifies specific details that we may wish to draw attention to, sheet two the teaching plan itself.

In addition, a completed example of a Year 6 gymnastic lesson can also be found that models how such plans can be completed.

Planning is usually best divided into different phases or parts (often three or four) to break up the time in order to use it most effectively. The examples are four part lessons using key words such as connect, activate, demonstrate and consolidate to provide direction and structure.

CONNECT
Sets out the physical and educational plan of the lesson. During this stage recap prior learning, establish the learning objective of the session and consider where resources need to be located.

ACTIVATE

Get the children moving by using an appropriate warm up and/or introductory activity. New skills can also be taught here.

DEMONSTRATE

This section requires the pupils to demonstrate to themselves and others that they can meet the learning outcomes. Examples can be the application of newly learned skills in a game through to the sharing of newly constructed sequences in gymnastics.

CONSOLIDATE

Always allow time to complete this part of the lesson properly, rather than just to clear up. Aim to create an opportunity for pupils to reflect upon 'what they were learning to do' (objectives) and how effectively they were met 'what you were looking for' (outcomes). If the session was particularly intensive an additional 'cool down' activity may also be appropriate to include.

Physical Education Lesson Plan

Class:	Date:
Activity:	Focus:
No. of pupils:	Sequence:
Location:	Time:

Intended outcomes:

All pupils will be able to:

Some pupils will be able to:

Few pupils will be able to:

Response to evaluation from previous lesson:

Equipment and resources (inc. use of support staff):

Health & Safety considerations:

Lit, Num, ICT, SMSC, any other notes.

Task / Time / Organisation	Objectives/ Teaching Points	Effective Learning Opportunities For All Pupils/ Outcomes (All, Some, Few)	Assessment Indicators
Connect:			
Activate:			
Demonstrate:			
Consolidate:			

Task / Time / Organisation	Objectives/ Teaching Points	Effective Learning Opportunities For All Pupils	Assessment Indicators
CONNECT - 5 mins State learning objective of the session Recap prior learning - lesson part of series Previous skills reviewed Setting out equipment	Clarify expectations. Key elements of forward and backward roll, take- off and landing. Safety points of working with partners. Follow instructions for safe handling of mats and apparatus.	All: pupils understand the focus of the lesson. Some: question areas of learning.	Q + A – recap previous lesson regarding forward & backward rolls. All: understand basic concept. Some: question effectiveness of the lesson.
ACTIVATE 1 - Warm Up - 10 mins Cardio-vascular warm-up. Pupils move around gym, in pairs, shadowing each other. Work on toes, with flexed knees, varied stride length, take off and land. Start slowly and increase pace. Front person jogs, slows down and stops. Front person builds body tension and lets him/herself drop backwards slightly for partner to support and put upright again. Lead stretching of relevant body parts, back, arms/shoulders, legs.	Mobilise joints. Preparation of working temperature of muscles. Re-cap of and preparation for taking off and landing for jumps. Building co-operation and trust. Communication between partners. Emphasise need for body tension and responsibility of supporter. Emphasise to the children where they should feel specific stretches.	All: copy and understand actions and follow instructions. Some: provide demonstrations. Few: Show excellent body tension and clear shape.	All: On task and involved in the warm up. Some: Allowing themselves to drop further to partner. Few: Can explain what parts of the body are being stretched and why.

Task / Time / Organisation	Objectives/ Teaching Points	Effective Learning Opportunities For All Pupils	Assessment Indicators
ACTIVATE 2 – Sequence preparation – 20-25mins Pupils practise and explore different types of rolls, and simple combinations with jumps, using apparatus, mats and partners to plan and practise sequence. Pupils may adapt/shape and change elements of their work area in negotiation with teacher.	Body shape clear. Hand position & how it changes for forward and backward rolls. Collaboration during sequences. Dynamic movement – how to achieve more flight. Timing - How can performance be improved?	Vary pupil groupings to have a mix of abilities giving the opportunity to learn from others and help others. Pupils work in pairs in their areas. Highlight the need for managing work area or, if necessary taking turns, to avoid risk of collisions. Encourage pupils to analyse work – identify improvements that can be made.	Pupils are visibly 'on-task'. Communication & negotiation is evident. Pupils use all of the space on offer. All are able to put a basic sequence together. Some have dynamic movements and link the sequence well. Few show real clarity and control in a well-timed sequence.
DEMONSTRATE – Demonstration of sequences – 10mins Class split into 2 – half to perform, the other half watch. Those watching must pick one pair to watch.	What can you see that is good? Identify 2 things. What can you see that needs improving? Identify 1 or 2 things. Use word wall – If struggling to feedback use word wall to help construct sentences e.g. flight.	Pupils perform sequences they have – emphasise that this is not the finished product. Half a group at a time eases the pressure of being watched and allows time for others to evaluate performances.	All pupils perform basic sequences to the best of their ability. Some have a clear starting and finishing position and include some dynamic movements. Few have clarity of movement, show good timing and perform most moves dynamically.
CONSOLIDATE – Feedback - 5 mins Feedback to pair you were watching **Equipment away & change – 5 mins**	Pairs offer feedback of key points to teacher. Write key points from feedback on board for start of next lesson.	Allow pairing within friendship groups for this lesson, change for future lessons.	All pupils are able to communicate & feedback effectively what they have learned. Some pupils offer more than suggested number of points. A few offer ideas about what they would like to improve in the future.

THE START OF THE LESSON

ESTABLISH ROUTINES

Well rehearsed routines enable effective class management and prevent lessons from becoming sidetracked from the learning experiences they are intended to be. Nowhere is this more apparent than at the beginning of a PE lesson. The fact that kit needs to be collected and changed into, jewellery removed and children need to move from one location to another provides ample opportunity for some to drift off task. Developing effective routines sends a clear message of expectation and consistency and can save precious time that should be spent on participating in a PE lesson.

THE LESSON STARTS IN THE CLASSROOM

A mistake that inexperienced practitioners make is believing that the PE lesson starts only when the class actually arrive in the area where the activity takes place e.g. when the children sit down in the hall or run on to the field. The fact is, that so much can and indeed should be established before arrival.

Firstly, establish areas where children can change. This should be away from public gaze and away from areas such as corridors where movement of others may take place. Also, make a sensible judgement as and when boys and girls need to change separately. Most children seem relatively comfortable in Year 4 and below in the same space but beyond that, two locations may be needed. In cases where children may feel self conscience, a sensible dialogue between child, parent/guardian and teacher can usually find an amicable solution.

Secondly, remind children of the expectations of the lesson they are taking part in. This could relate to prior learning, quality of movement or even just how to walk from the classroom to the school hall and what to do upon arrival!

IDENTIFY AND SHARE OBJECTIVES

Inexperienced teachers and trainees often get confused between learning objectives and learning outcomes. All too often we as teachers can identify what we want to see and will know when we see it, (an outcome), but are not always as specific as we might be at articulating precisely what we are doing (an objective) or indeed how the two are different. A sure way of defining an objective is to complete the phrase, 'we are learning to….' Once we have worked out what we are learning to do in the lesson, we can plan it effectively.

Sharing the objectives of the lesson with the class is also of prime importance. Not only does this provide a focus for everyone (both teacher and class) about what they are learning to do, but enables the children themselves to evaluate how successful they have been in achieving their objective.

SHARE EXPECTATIONS/OUTCOMES

Another important matter to share is what we expect to see in the lesson. This can cover more general points, such as behaviour and teamwork but should also identify outcomes that link to the learning objective. Again, a most effective way of defining an outcome is the completion of a phrase, this time, 'what I'm looking for is....' Once we have worked out what we are looking for we can also engage more readily in any form of assessment.

CLEAR CONCISE INSTRUCTIONS

Nothing will test a teacher's ability more than to communicate clearly and concisely to children who are spread out across a large open space. Avoid trying to give too many instructions and if lots of information does need to be shared, then break up the delivery of points by spacing them out over the session. Also, try and be precise about the wording used. If children are told simply to 'get a ball', then don't be surprised if they take liberties on the way back e.g. roll it, bounce it, kick it. If as a teacher, you didn't want this to happen, always ask yourself 'Why did it happen?'. The truth is, that most of the time it is because exactly what was required was not communicated clearly enough. Ultimately, precision and clarity of what is required saves a lot of time for both teachers and children alike.

RECAP LINKS WITH PRIOR LEARNING

As PE sessions are most commonly taught once or twice per week in Primary schools, it is always important to reflect on prior learning. Some children will have forgotten key points of previous lessons (or may have been absent) and will need reminding of the important information. If in doubt use objectives and outcomes of earlier sessions, as this should have been the foundation on which the current lesson is built.

INVOLVE NON PARTICIPANTS

For a variety of reasons, children may not be able to take part in a PE lesson on a given day e.g. minor injury, lack of kit etc. Should this be the case, it does not mean that such children should not play an active part in the session.

Involving them as assistants will not only serve to include them, which is better for both them and the teacher but if focused appropriately e.g. asked to help others evaluate and improve their performance, such children can prove to be a most effective resource.

WARMING UP

Warm ups are often something that teachers feel they have to do rather than use them effectively as part of the foundation on which a successful lesson is to be built. The trick to selecting an effective warm up activity is to identify exactly what its purpose is. In that respect, there are three kinds that begin to emerge, of which one (sometimes two on a cold day) can be selected.

The first type that could be selected is the 'run around game' which aims to be fun, raises the heart rate and mimics the movement of the main activity. Such examples include 'tag games' such as 'stuck in the mud' which are ideal warm ups for invasion games in which children will be moving around each other in a given space.

The second type still seeks to get the body 'warmed up' but this is in combination with stretching with its focus and aims to be much more calm, serious, specific and controlled. Such examples include 'directed' running e.g. shuttles followed by a whole body stretching routine. This is particularly useful for activities such as athletics or gymnastics which may focus on specific parts of the body and therefore need a 'specific warm up'.

The third and final choice that could be made is more akin to an introductory activity. Here, specific skills to be used through the session, ideally from prior sessions, can be reinforced. Such examples would include individual racket skills for tennis or throwing and catching for rounders and enables the teacher to focus children quickly into what is to be learned.

In this book, ideas for warm ups can be taken from the short activities identified in part 2.

START SLOWLY AND BUILD

When children begin a session of PE, it is often after a longer period of inactivity (such as sitting in a classroom), so it is important that the session builds steadily from the start, through the warm up and into the main activities, rather than go 'flat out' from the start. As children exercise they tire quickly. The significance of this is that the level of performance in any given skill will decline the more tired they become, so it is often a good idea to address the 'acquiring and developing' of skills earlier in the session to facilitate higher quality work in this specific strand.

GETTING THE EQUIPMENT

This aspect of the lesson is far more difficult than it first appears and is often an issue that less experienced teachers don't give enough attention to. Ultimately, the problem to solve is after working out what equipment is needed, how to make it available and accessible for the children to use. Expecting a class of thirty children to all get a ball from the same box at the same time is always going to end in tears, so credible solutions have to be found. There are of course many ways to solve this but they have to be well managed and slick, or else the pace of the session can be lost and children drift off task. The other extreme, for example, of one child at a time getting a piece of equipment is equally problematic.

Putting equipment around the wall, such as small piles of hockey sticks or a line of basketballs, is a simple yet manageable way to spread out resources so that children can get them more easily.

On an additional point, always make sure the equipment needed is there (e.g. the correct number of balls) and is in appropriate condition (e.g. that balls are sufficiently inflated).

DEFINE THE SPACE

A regular comment made by those inspecting PE lessons, including OFSTED, is the poor organisation and use of space shown by non specialist teachers. A good working use of the space is essential to underpin the activities that will transpire during the lesson, so thought should be given to how areas are best defined.

Identify and then communicate the external perimeter of the space. In a school hall this is very straight forward as the walls already define the edges. That said, it should be stressed that the space cannot be left without permission. Outside, defining the perimeter can be more difficult but is arguably more important, as children need to know clearly, for instance, how far they can move across a large field. In many cases, premarked lines can be used but in the absence of such, natural barriers can often be utilised, such as fences or trees. If obvious choices are not available then the use of markers is best employed. Some tall, well placed, high visibility cones should easily communicate where children should and should not go.

The establishing of an area to which children can be brought back to is also of vital importance, as it provides a focal point for the class to return to whenever further instruction needs to be given. Existing lines and markers can again be used to define the area, it is important that the 'shape' chosen allows a space where children can gather together for corralling purposes but also allows them to stand around in order to watch a demonstration.

A semi circle is ideal for this, with the class standing around the curve whilst the teacher stands at the flat side with the resources to be used. This arrangement allows each child a good line of site, provides a space for demonstration and explanation and enables the teacher to maintain eye contact with all pupils. On a windy day too, the arc of children can provide a natural shelter to the smaller teaching space and means that voices do not have to be raised above the elements.

The space to be used for activity should be also used intelligently. If high levels of activity are required then maximise the space, but if close skill work is needed where pupils need to learn greater control e.g. dribbling a basketball, then smaller areas work well. For small sided games, divide the space equally e.g. 30 children fit nicely into 3 games of 5 v 5, or 32 children fit easily into 4 games of 4 v 4.

THE MAIN PART OF THE LESSON

EFFECTIVE COMMUNICATION

To communicate key points effectively, it is imperative to get the attention of everyone in the group. As indicated previously, defining an area such as a semi circle allows each child a good line of site, provides a space for demonstration and explanation and enables the teacher to maintain eye contact with all pupils

Once all are gathered and focused, communicate clearly the learning objectives for the session – What are they learning to do? Why? If possible have these visible (perhaps on a whiteboard) to provide a focus to the learning.

DEMONSTRATIONS

If a 'picture says a thousand words' then the power of demonstration is obvious. The most important aspect is making sure that the demonstrations are of high quality. If as a teacher you show accurately how something should be done, you have every right to expect that the children should copy. That said, if the demonstration is poor, then the children will copy this too.

In instances where it is considered that a high quality demonstration cannot be given by you as the teacher, it is often possible to find a child who may be able to show something better. But remember, the pupil selected must be doing the basics correctly, allowing you to point out the key teaching points as they perform. Also, it may seem a small point but try to remember to thank any pupils that help in this way – they do appreciate it.

TEACHING POINTS

In practical lessons, with so much going on, it is easy to forget the main teaching points of the session - yet obviously, this is the most important aspect. Key things to do here are to firstly identify the main teaching points on the planning. Secondly, make sure you are clear how points link to both the objective and the outcomes. Thirdly refer to them during the lesson and ideally again in the plenary to reinforce and if in doubt, choose less teaching points in order to communicate simply and effectively. Lastly, have a written reminder of key points visible during a lesson, this can be on a whiteboard or even just in your pocket.

ENCOURAGE PUPILS TO PERFORM

To develop the evaluation and improvement strand it is good practice to allow pupils the opportunity to perform for each other during a session. If this is done regularly it ceases to be an intimidating situation, especially if for instance, half the class performs for the other half. Comments can then be encouraged to identify something that they liked in another pupils performance and highlight something that they could develop further.

TRANSITIONS AND GETTING INTO GROUPS

As mentioned previously, ineffective transitions can ruin a lesson, not least when asking children to get into groups. What seems such an innocuous request can delay lessons needlessly. In short, specific instructions are needed and are most effective if a matter of urgency is created. Expecting an instruction of 'quickly get yourselves into groups of four' is one thing but expecting them to sit down and show you they are ready by the time you have counted to five is quite another.

Coloured bands or equipment can also help here. Bands can even be given out before the lesson starts and later coloured groups can be formed on request. Similarly, if children are playing with different coloured equipment, such as beanbags, those who are using the same colour can then follow a specific instruction to work together.

It is also a good idea not to allow children to pick their own groups, especially in games, as the dynamics that are created may not be conducive to the learning environment you were trying to create. Though some pupils may complain at first, if it is usual practice, they will soon stop asking.

MOVEMENT AROUND GROUPS

Generally, it makes sense during a session to try to visit each pupil/group/area. This can often go wrong if not planned for. Consciously move from one to another in a pre planned way (clockwise, groups 1 – 4 etc.). Where possible maintain good lines of sight, moving around the outside of the room or be located at one edge. If working with a group in the centre of the room, take a position that will give you the best view of most of the rest and then move out to the periphery from time to time to get a broader perspective.

ALLOW ADEQUATE TIME FOR PUPILS TO PRACTISE

In order to fit in all the different sections of a lesson, (all the teaching points, questions and demonstrations) the temptation is to keep stopping and starting the class. Though this will need to happen as the lesson progresses, it is important to allow sufficient time for children to practise and develop what has been asked of them. If the session stops every two minutes, little development can actually take place.

In addition, it is not uncommon for the quality of pupil performance to dip once they have been taught something new. Again, the temptation is to stop the lesson and recorrect (which is the right thing to do if they have completely misunderstood) but in many cases, all that needs to occur is sufficient time for the children to practise and develop their skills.

GIVING FEEDBACK

As teachers, we often give lots of encouraging feedback, such as 'well done' or 'that was really good' but not always as much specific feedback as we should. By following such statements with an explanation as to 'why' something was good, not only does it encourage pupils but it also reinforces the teaching points e.g. 'that sequence was really good - you linked all the different movements together so it looked really smooth.'

IDENTIFY SELECTED PUPILS

Before the lesson started pupils should have been identified for specific reasons e.g. SEN, Gifted & Talented, Assessment Focus (see, before the lesson). Remember to locate where these children are and to give them the intended attention, such as the right question or a recorded observation. As with teaching points, if you are worried you will forget, write it down.

INTERVENTIONS

A regular criticism of non specialist PE teachers by many external inspections, is that they manage a PE session but do not actually do any teaching. This appears to be because they do not actually know what to do or say. The simple remedy to this is to look closely at what is going on in the lesson and ask yourself, 'Is this good enough? Is this what I wanted?' If the answer is 'NO', then take a moment to assess what is wrong and then intervene. This could be speaking to just one child or stopping the whole session. If such scanning of a group seems too daunting, pick one or two children who you know are an honest representation of the class and look closely at what they are doing. Remember, time must be planned for (just like Literacy and Numeracy) in which the teacher will teach not only in whole class situations but with small groups and identified individuals also.

VOICE, WHISTLES and ACOUSTICS

As teachers we know that our voice is the most important teaching tool that we have. Varying the pitch of our voices to praise, motivate and control behaviour is something that seems to become second nature after a short while in the job. However, in larger environments such as sports halls or out on the playground it is very easy for our voices not be heard or worse to become overstrained in a bid to be heard over a long distance.

In buildings such as gyms and sports halls, acoustics can vary enormously, so the first thing to do is identify where the better places to stand would be when needing to be heard e.g. away from a road. If nowhere obvious seems apparent try speaking to a group near a wall or corner. Ideally, it would make sense to establish the 'shape' (see 'define the space') in such an area to maximise effective communication in the teaching space.

If needing to get attention over a longer distance, whistles are an appropriate tool to use but make sure they are not overused – especially indoors! If the voice needs to be projected over a longer distance, the temptation is to shout from the throat which can very quickly be quite sore. The most effective way by far is to take a deep breath first and then project outwards pushing from the diaphragm. This will be considerably louder! Remember that the sound will be loudest in the direction the mouth is pointing so make sure you are facing the most appropriate direction.

One final point to make here is that some activities produce a large amount of noise e.g. a class of thirty children all bouncing a basketball. Regardless of strength of voice, some children simply won't respond immediately if asked to 'stop' because of the noise. One mechanism that may help is to use the voice in an exaggerated way, so instead of simply saying 'stop' very loudly the alternative would be to say 'aaaaaaaaand stop'. The length of sound not only breaks through the noise more effectively but allows even the most unaware child longer to realise that everyone else has stopped!

PUPIL POSITIONING

Pupils can often become easily distracted outdoors so thought needs to be given to where they are located when listening to the teacher. The two often overlooked factors here are wind and sun.

The importance of a teacher's voice and their ability to project is discussed above. However, outside, this will be even more important and can be influenced markedly by the direction of the wind. If in doubt always project downwind (with the wind behind) as the sound will travel further.

Secondly, make sure that pupils are not looking into the sun. Lots of squinting eyes and hands shielding the sun is not conducive to concentration. The only person that may have to do this is you as the teacher but that is preferable over the rest of the class.

ASSESSMENT FOR LEARNING

When the word assessment is mentioned many teachers think of record keeping, tests or report writing. Much of what is recorded is assessment of learning or summative assessments occurring at the end of a period of time i.e. term or school year. Though such records are useful indicators to tracking long term progress, they are not much use in indicating what a pupil needs to do next in order to improve.

To do this, Assessment for Learning or Formative Assessment should be employed. It relies on teachers actively observing learning taking place, analysing and interpreting evidence of learning and then giving appropriate feedback so that pupils will improve and achieve their aim.

To make this task manageable, a small number of children can be focused upon at any one time, with key questions directed to them in order to ascertain their level of understanding (see, before the lesson starts).

INCLUSION

In short, there is no good reason why every child in your class should not be included in every activity you plan – it is their legal entitlement. There is also no good reason why boys and girls should not be equally involved in all PE activities. Netball is not the exclusive preserve for girls and football is not the exclusive preserve for boys. Such cultures may evolve but consider what you and your school do to reinforce or challenge such cultures.

ANTICIPATE

Though it is never possible to predict every eventuality that is likely to occur in every lesson, it is possible to anticipate events that are likely to happen. For instance, if you give a child a coloured band or bib to identify which team/group they are in, it is almost a certainty that they will put it on without being asked (try it!). What if, as a teacher you didn't want this to happen? Are you surprised? Frustrated? Annoyed? This may seem trivial but highlights a type of behaviour that could have been anticipated. Such an instance can often occur, so take time to think 'what will you do if…?'

PHYSICAL ACTIVITY SHOULD NEVER BE A PUNISHMENT

Many adults have been put off exercise due to bad experiences they had in PE and sport, whilst at school. One common reason is that engaging in physical activity was used as something that had to be endured, had to hurt and was sometimes used as a punishment. It is imperative that such messages are avoided and that PE is an activity area within which all can feel valued and make progress.

THE END OF THE LESSON

WARMING DOWN

If the session has been particularly intensive, it is a good idea to engage in a warming down activity. As a rule of thumb, consider how the lesson has placed demands on the body and plan a warm down that represents similar slower, lower key movements. For example, provide walking or jogging activities for sessions involving lots of running.

WHAT HAVE THEY LEARNED?

The plenary is the appropriate time for children to reflect upon what they have learned and for the teacher to reinforce important teaching points. As indicated earlier, this is an ideal opportunity to ask key questions and to target specific pupils identified at the start of the lesson.

WHAT NEXT?

To make sense of where each lesson fits in and relates to the next step, it is often a good idea to indicate to children what is coming next and why. Such communication indicates a clear structure to learning but allows the children to see how they are progressing.

COLLECT EQUIPMENT

Collecting equipment should not be an onerous task. Children love to help and so by dividing up the equipment between specific children or groups, effective collection should be possible, providing instructions are clear. Always remember, however, that another member of staff is going to follow, so ensure that everything is put away properly.

GETTING BACK

What was true of getting to the lesson is also true of returning to the classroom. The session does not finish the moment the activity is over and standards must be maintained when moving between areas such as from the school hall back to the classroom.

AFTER THE LESSON

COMPLETE LESSON EVALUATION

The most effective practitioners continually reflect and evaluate their work. Making simple notes or annotating lesson plans is often sufficient for such a task but for less experienced individuals a more structured approach is often advisable.

Below is an example of a lesson evaluation including prompts for reflection, followed by a specific example to demonstrate what might be written.

Lesson Evaluation:

Has learning taken place?

Have your planned outcomes been met fully, partially or not at all? Why?

Did you feel your planned outcomes met the needs of all pupils?

What teaching strategies did you adopt that worked, didn't work?

How effective was your organisation?

How did pupils respond to the tasks set?

Example Evaluation

This lesson went reasonably well and the learning objectives were on the whole achieved. The majority of pupils were engaged and working co-operatively with each other. All pupils put together sequences that involved elements of forward and backward rolling. The majority of students performed backward rolls without active assistance, although two pupils (Daniel and Ryan) needed some assistance to do this. Pupils also used the given apparatus and mats creatively, using benches for instance to perform rolls on. The quality of movement varied significantly between the more able and less able pupils. The elements that included partner work were particularly enjoyed. One pair included a roll over a bench, introducing timing as another variable. The elements of group work were particularly successful and some of the final displays demonstrated creativity as well as skill. Pupils provided on-going feedback to each other and the final discussion brought out some factors that make the quality of a performance, such as speed, fluency, body shape/tension and creativity.

The warm-up did not go as well as I had hoped. I feel that this was mainly due to the fact that there was not sufficient space in the gym, after we had set up the equipment. I think I should have been quicker to adjust, when I realised this. I will therefore have to consider space implications in more detail, when planning for the introductory part of the session, or perhaps change the sequence and set up the equipment after the first activity.

Most pupils were able to contribute feedback to the pair whose sequence they had observed though this varied in quality. A list of key areas for improvement was made from the feedback and will be used to start the next lesson.

COMPLETE ASSESSMENTS

Always find the time to record any assessments that have been made. Though the common excuse given is that "there isn't time", the truth is that there is time, if you want to make time for it. Recording does not have to be elaborate, but should be habitual and easy to do. One quick and easy method to use is to have a small notepad and pen (or more than one) that is located in a relevant place. This can be organised into subjects, areas or even children's names and when something relevant is to be recorded, it can be jotted down whilst still fresh in the mind. Such recording is preferable over any matrix or tick list, as any comments made are always far more specific and meaningful about the child concerned.

REVIEW NEXT LESSON

Sometimes, lessons will be devised in detail in advance. Unfortunately children do not progress uniformly and so it is always important to review what is to be taught next, in light of what happened in the previous lesson. Where the next planned lesson fails to meet the needs of the pupils, the only effective course of action is to replan the lesson.

STORING EQUIPMENT

It is important that when PE equipment is not being used it is stored securely and separately. Not only does this stop balls 'wandering off' and thereby ensuring that the appropriate amount is available for teaching but sets an important example that this equipment is for a specific task and should be looked after properly.

EXTRA CURRICULAR LINKS

Though it may not be explicitly the role of a teacher to be involved in sporting extra curricular activities, it is still important to support and promote something that links so easily with Physical Education. This does not have to be direct involvement, as teachers may not have the time or the inclination to offer such activities, but through indirect action such as encouraging children to attend. The most obvious example is identifying a particularly able performer who as yet has no other outlet for what they do.

PART TWO

Activity Ideas

INVASION GAMES

Presently, Invasion Games undoubtedly get more attention than any area within a school's PE curriculum and often these are taught as discreet 'sports' such as football, netball or hockey. As a result of the sports focus in schools, which in recent years has been encouraged by successive governments and initiatives such as TOP Sport, there has been a tendency to teach (or more accurately coach!) the skills associated with a specific sport. Though such skills clearly have a place, it's important to stress these are not the 'be all and end all' of games teaching and should not lead the planning but rather be inserted into a programme led by sound principles e.g. What is the most effective way to win a point? Where should I move in order to receive the next pass? One key point that should be highlighted here, as can be seen from the summarised programmes of study outlined in the PE National Curriculum for Key Stages 1 and 2 shown below, is that the use of small sided and modified games is specified as a preferred mode of delivery.

Key Stage 1:

Pupils should be taught to:
a.   travel with, send and receive a ball and other equipment in different ways

b.   develop these skills for simple net, striking/fielding and invasion-type games

c.   play simple, competitive net, striking/fielding and invasion-type games that they and others have made, using simple tactics for attacking and defending.

Key Stage 2:

Pupils should be taught to:
a.   play and make up small-sided and modified competitive net, striking/fielding and invasion games

b.   use skills and tactics and apply basic principles suitable for attacking and defending

c.   work with others to organise and keep the games going.

The ideas here are focused upon netball and basketball as a vehicle for this area, as it is possibly the area that Primary schools are best equipped to provide (though it is relatively easy to apply the same principles to other invasion games that schools may have provision for such as football or hockey). The lesson ideas provided are linked to the following QCA Schemes of work for Physical Education:

> **Year 1 & 2:   (Unit 4) Games Activities 2**
>
> **Year 3 & 4:   (Unit 11) Invasion Games 2**
>
> **Year 5 & 6:   (Unit 24) Invasion Games 4**

KEY POINTS FOR IMPLEMENTATION

When delivering effective Invasion Games in Primary school there are three fundamental principles that need to be considered:

Develop individual confidence by having lots of time with equipment

Nothing develops confidence more during a games session than having command over the equipment being used. Though for many this has often been interpreted as doing lots of skills practices, it need not be the case. Giving a child five minutes guided play for example with a ball at the start of every session will reap considerable benefits in terms of control, far beyond anything that repetitive drills could develop.

Develop fundamentals using small sided games

Though an activity being used may be a recognised sporting form such as football, it must always be remembered that the full adult version is not appropriate for Primary age pupils. Children do not have the physiological development to run extensive distances and what is more, in a large sided game such as eleven or eight a-side, pupils do not get enough time making decisions or gaining touches with the ball to develop their confidence learned from above. During any kind of competitive play, a considerable amount of time should be spent developing principles in 3 v 3 or 4 v 4 situations.

Remember to teach and not just manage

It is easy to be satisfied once the children have been organised into teams to simply allow them to 'get on with it'. However, it is important to remember to keep teaching them rather than to simply manage the activity (a regular criticism from OFSTED). Opportunities can be found at many different times during a session to demonstrate or give specific teaching points, but if natural breaks seem not to be obvious then don't be afraid simply to stop or 'freeze' a game and ask questions such as 'Show me where you should run next? Why?' Teaching within a game situation may seem an alien concept but to facilitate aspects such as passing and moving there is simply no better way.

ACTIVITIES FOR YEARS 1 & 2

Children should learn:
- to improve the way they coordinate and control their bodies and a range of equipment
- to remember, repeat and link combinations of skills
- to choose, use and vary simple tactics

Walkabout

Resources – One ball per child

Task – Staying in control, bounce a ball and then take it for a walk whilst bouncing it. Remember to encourage children to keep their heads up as much as possible and to use both left and right hands.

Traffic Lights

Resources – One ball per child

Task – Ask children to follow the commands of Red, Amber and Green and perform different tasks on different colours e.g. Red = Hold the ball still in two hands, Amber = Bounce the ball on the spot, Green = Take the ball for a walk.

Duck

Resources – One ball per group of four

Task – Three children stand in a line, one behind the other, facing towards the person with the ball. The person with the ball, passes to the front of the line, who then returns the ball. Each time this is successful the child at the front ducks down. This is repeated until all have ducked down and then the positions can be rotated.

Beat Your Score

Resources – One ball per pair

Task – In pairs, children attempt to pass the ball quickly to each other and complete as many passes as possible in a short time e.g. 30 seconds. To encourage the concept of getting better with practice a quick cheat is to allow them another chance to improve but secretly give them 40 seconds the second time instead of 30!

Catch Me If You Can

Resources – One ball per group of eight

Task – Eight children make a circle and warm up by passing a ball around the circle (in sequence). Then another ball is included and passed around. The task is to try and make one ball catch up with the other.

Piggy in the Middle

Resources – One ball per group of three

Task – A classic but an important step in decision making. A pair of children attempt to pass the ball to each other whilst a 'piggy' in the middle attempts to stop them. Give both the pairs and the piggy a score to aim for e.g. 10 passes or 2 blocks.

'Shooting Hoops'

Resources – One ball per pair and a scattering of large hoops

Task – In pairs, children move around the hooped area and score points by passing the ball to each other by bouncing it in a hoop. As children progress they can be encouraged to stand further away or to use one hand.

Endball

Resources – One ball per group of six

Task – Arrange groups into 3 v 3, playing in a small area. Don't allow children to run with the ball or to tackle. Each team should try and pass the ball through their area and score by throwing the ball against a wall or throwing it over a line (in other words very large goals!). Additional rules maybe required but try not to add them unless absolutely necessary.

ACTIVITIES FOR YEARS 3 & 4

Children should learn:
- to improve their ability to choose and use simple tactics and strategies
- to devise and use rules
- to use and adapt tactics in different situations

Slalom Dribble

Resources – One ball per team/pair, cones

Task – In turn each child negotiates a number of gates/cones whilst dribbling a ball and then swaps with the next person. This activity can be raised or lowered to vary the competitive aspects but a key consideration is not to have too many in a queue.

Runaround

Resources – One ball per group of eight

Task - Eight children make a circle and warm up by passing a ball around the circle (in sequence). Then one child who is the designated starter attempts to run around the outside of the group before the ball can be passed around the circle. The larger the circle the harder children will have to work.

15 Up!

Resources – One ball per child/pair, large cones and/or hoops

Task – Individually or in pairs, children travel around an area and score points for shooting into hoops or hitting skittles. Once a score such as 15 has been achieved, the game is replayed. Again different rules can be applied and in this case to different children e.g. more able have to use their less dominant hand to shoot.

Triangles

Resources – One ball per group of three

Task – In threes (triangle shape) children demonstrate a range of different passes. Specific skills such as bounce passes etc. can be inserted when appropriate. Encourage children to change direction, so that the ball doesn't always go the same way.

Tag Dribble

Resources – One ball per child

Task – Children dribble around in a small area and three appointed children attempt to tag their ball. The purpose is for each to defend/shield the ball by turning and changing direction. As children progress the 'taggers' can have a ball too. To differentiate further, the game can be played in small groups of similar ability with seven dribblers and one chaser.

Lineball

Resources – One ball per group of six

Task – Arrange groups into a 3 v 3, playing in a small area. Don't allow children to run with the ball or to tackle. Each team should try and pass the ball through their area and score by touching the ball down (as in rugby) over a line. Again, additional rules may be required but try not to add them unless absolutely necessary. At this stage try and 'teach within the game' and ask questions such as 'Can you point to a space?' and 'Where should you move next?' The key aim is to work at preventing the herding that occurs at this age. If you don't teach them good principles of where to move they'll just follow the ball.

Hoopball/Skittleball

Resources – One ball per group of six

Task – As above but instead the aim is to score by shooting the ball into a hoop on the floor or hitting a skittle. This step, as well as encouraging accuracy of shooting, will see children develop the principle of defence over time as they aim to protect their hoop or skittle. Should this occur, look for ways to modify the game with the children e.g. mark out an area around the target or have targets (which don't have to always be placed at the end of an area).

Overload 1

Resources – One ball per group of four

Task – Without dribbling, a group of three children attempt to pass the ball through an area whilst one defender aims to tag the ball. Targets can be given for the number of successful attempts or successful tags.

ACTIVITIES FOR YEARS 5 & 6

Children should learn:
- to choose, combine and perform skills more fluently and effectively in invasion games
- to understand, choose and apply a range of tactics and strategies for defence and attack
- to use these tactics and strategies more consistently in similar games

Pass and Follow

Resources – One ball per group of eight

Task – Eight children make a circle and warm up by passing a ball across the circle. Once a ball is passed the child should follow it across the circle. Children should be encouraged to make eye contact and call each other's name before passing. As a group becomes more proficient another ball is included and children should be encouraged to make good decisions about when to run, stop or pass.

Passing Squares

Resources – One ball per group of four/five

Task – In fours (square shape) children demonstrate a range of different passes. Specific skills such as shoulder passes etc. can be used when appropriate. Encourage children to change direction, so that the ball doesn't always go the same way. As soon as children are used to this, put pressure on their passes by asking another child to try and chase the ball.

Caterpillars

Resources – One ball per group of six

Task – In groups of six (standing in two lines), children attempt to pass a ball from one line to another. Once a pass has been made the passer runs to the other end of the line ready to receive the ball again once it has zigzagged along. Competition can be added by racing caterpillars against each other.

Alley Dribble

Resources – One ball per child, markers

Task – In small groups, children attempt to dribble a ball through a narrow area, from one end to another. Two children, near either end attempt to tag the ball of anyone running through. Encourage children not to turn back but to beat the defender with a specific skill or change of direction.

Conditioned Games e.g. Possession Ball

Resources – One ball per group of six/eight

Task – Arrange groups into a 3 v 3 or 4 v 4 playing in a small area. To develop specific principles, games should be 'conditioned' where different teams are given different rules. For instance, one team could be trying to play and score as normal during a game of skittle ball, where their opponents are merely trying to keep possession of the ball and count the number of passes. Similarly some games may involve dribbling, others may not and rules can be imposed so that all have to touch the ball. This is a key step in developing high quality games play and should be used with key groups or individuals to differentiate their learning.

Overload 2

Resources – One ball per group of six/eight

Task – Without dribbling, a group of four/five children attempt to pass the ball through an area whilst two/three defenders aims to tag the ball. Targets can be given for the number of successful attempts or successful tags. This activity can also be played by dividing an area into zones e.g. 2 v 1 in each zone.

4 v 4 Various Games

Resources – One ball per group of eight, various equipment

Task – As hoopball/skittleball/possession ball (see previous). It is always important to have one eye on the end point of Key Stage 2 and in the case of invasion games, the best foundation for Key Stage 3 is to be able to play a variety of invasion games, whether netball, hockey, football etc. in competitive 4 v 4 situations. Though it may be tempting to encourage children into 5 v 5 or 7 v 7 situations in PE, which replicates 'adult' basketball or netball, the extra learning that takes place in 4 v 4 cannot be underestimated.

NET/WALL GAMES

Activities such as Tennis, Badminton, Table Tennis, Squash and Volleyball are included in this bracket and are traditionally difficult to deliver in many Primary schools because of the demand they place upon equipment, space or both. Anyone who has attempted to provide a quality tennis lesson using half a dozen randomly sized rackets with thirty-two children in a school hall, who all want to hit a ball, will appreciate the difficulties. It is understandable why Net/Wall games have not received so much attention, though in recent years the Top Sport initiative has seen much more equipment in Primary schools to support this area.

One key point that should be highlighted here, as can be seen from the summarised programmes of study outlined in the PE National Curriculum for Key Stage 1 and 2 shown below, is that elements to address include the development of tactics and not just a focus upon skills, as is often the case with this area.

Key Stage 1:

Pupils should be taught to:
a.   develop skills for simple net games
b.   play simple, competitive net type games that they and others have made, using simple tactics for attacking and defending.

Key Stage 2:

Pupils should be taught to:
a.   play and make up small-sided and modified competitive net games
b.   use skills and tactics and apply basic principles suitable for attacking and defending.

The ideas here are focused upon tennis as a vehicle for this area, as it is possibly the area that Primary schools are best equipped to provide (though it is relatively easy to apply the same principles to other net/wall games that schools may have provision for such as Table Tennis). The lesson ideas provided are linked to the following QCA Schemes of work for Physical Education:

> **Year 1 & 2:   (Unit 13) Net/Wall Games 1**
>
> **Year 3 & 4:   (Unit 13) Net/Wall Games 1**
>
> **Year 5 & 6:   (Unit 26) Net/Wall Games 2**

KEY POINTS FOR IMPLEMENTATION

When delivering enjoyable and effective net/wall games in Primary school there are three fundamental principles that need to be considered:

Consider the progression needed

When the Wimbledon Tennis Championship rolls around we are reminded again of what the pinnacle of a particular sport should look like. However, just because there are rackets in the PE store doesn't mean that using them in your next tennis lesson will be the most appropriate choice. Consideration must be given to playing games that will develop principles such as footwork, movement and placement before any ball is hit. This should include having the opportunity to 'pat' the ball over a barrier with a hand, an experience vital if a child is to appreciate the upwards hitting action required and the amount of power needed to return a ball.

Racket selection

Rackets found in Primary schools will usually include plastic ones which vary wildly in head and handle size, wooden ones which are often ridiculously heavy and metal rackets with strings which are so powerful they are hard to control or are so slack they could be used to catch fish! Given such choices, the aspect which seems to hamper children the most is a racket which has an over long handle and so where possible try to equip the store with short handled, light plastic rackets which are far easier to control at this stage.

Develop understanding of where to place a shot

Before attempting to hit a ball with a racket, it seems sensible to think that time should be spent on knowing where and how a ball should be placed. Simple games in pairs of throwing and catching a ball over a barrier can develop an awareness of how points can be won e.g. putting a ball into space, dropping the ball short. Once this aspect has been fostered tactical play becomes intrinsic, making children aware of what they are actually trying to do, rather than simply hit a ball.

In addition to the usual activities found in other activity areas, focused activities have also been included to demonstrate the appropriate progressions required as the children move through the school.

ACTIVITIES FOR YEARS 1 & 2

Children should learn:
- to consolidate and develop the range and consistency of their skills in net game
- to choose and use a range of simple tactics and strategies
- to keep, adapt and make rules for net games

Bounce, Clap, Catch

Resources – One ball per child

Task – Various challenges of bouncing, throwing and catching can be set but one of the most useful involves asking children to bounce a ball, clap their hands and catch the ball. The more able the child, the more times they can try and clap their hands.

Gone for a Walk

Resources – One ball and racket per child

Task – Holding the racket like a frying pan, place the ball on the face. Now simply take it for a walk without it falling off. Variations can include bouncing and walking or even a jog.

Caterpillar Rackets

Resources – One racket per child and one ball per team

Task – In teams of 6/8, standing in a line, children attempt to pass a ball from one racket to another without the ball falling to the floor. Children can be encouraged to run from the back to the front of their line ready to receive the ball again.

Keep It Up!

Resources – One ball and racket per child

Task – Holding the racket like a frying pan, children simply hit the ball in a controlled manner into the air and try to repeat this as many times as possible. Encourage children to remember their best score and try to beat this each time.

FOCUS ACTIVITIES

Progression 1

Individually, children throw a ball in the air or bounce a ball on the floor. Attention should be given to tracking the ball and catching confidently in two hands.

Progression 2

In pairs, children co-operatively throw and catch a ball to each other. The ball should be thrown underarm mimicking the arm swing in tennis and should bounce once before being caught.

Progression 3

The aim of the game is to score points by throwing a ball underarm into the opponent's court area and making it bounce twice. Play the game one against one. Use a low net, bench or even just a line to separate an area that will make a court area. Ask the children to choose their own way to start and restart the game. Play up to 3 points before starting a new game. During the activity ask children to consider 'what is the best way to win a point/make the ball bounce twice?' The use of pupil demonstration is vital to developing this level of understanding.

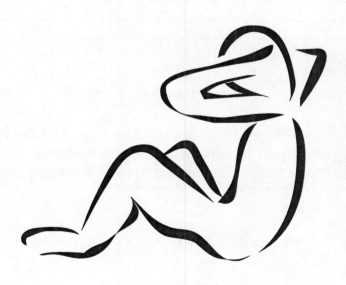

ACTIVITIES FOR YEARS 3 & 4

Children should learn:
- to consolidate and develop the range and consistency of their skills in net game
- to choose and use a range of simple tactics and strategies
- to keep, adapt and make rules for net games

Pancake Catch

Resources – One ball and racket per child

Task – Holding the racket like a frying pan, children throw their ball in the air and attempt to catch or balance the ball on the face of the racket again without it bouncing off.

It's a Knockout

Resources – One ball and racket per child

Task – Holding the racket like a frying pan, place the ball on the face. Children attempt to take the ball for a walk without it falling off. At the same time, nominated children are attempting to 'flick' balls off each racket. Caution must be taken to play this game sensibly.

Beat the Clock

Resources – One ball per pair

Task – Various challenges of bouncing, throwing, hitting and catching can be set including 'how many times can you pat a ball to each other in thirty seconds?'

Double Up

Resources – One ball per group

Task – In groups of 4, children attempt to learn how to play alternate shots in doubles play. At this stage, patting is the most desirable form of doubles play.

FOCUS ACTIVITIES

Progression 1

In pairs, children co-operatively throw and catch a ball to each other. The ball should be thrown underarm mimicking the arm swing in tennis and should bounce once before being caught.

Progression 2

The aim of the game is to score points by throwing a ball underarm into the opponent's court area and making it bounce twice. Play the game one against one. Use a low net, bench or even just a line to separate an area that will make a court area. Children should start their throw (or serve) from behind the back of the court (or baseline). Play up to 5 points before starting a new game. During the activity ask children to consider 'what is the best way to win a point/make the ball bounce twice?' The use of pupil demonstration is vital to developing this level of understanding.

Progression 3

The aim of the game is to score points by patting a ball underarm into the opponent's court area and making it bounce twice. Play the game one against one. Use a low net, bench or even just a line to separate an area that will make a court area. Children should throw the ball in to serve and from then onwards hit or 'pat' the ball with their hand over the net – mimicking the action of a racket. Play up to 5 points before starting a new game. Children will develop a real sense of control with this activity, which is vital before bringing in rackets. Naturally too, children will begin to use the back of their hand to hit the ball, which leads to fluidity of movement when developing backhand shots later on.

ACTIVITIES FOR YEARS 5 & 6

Children should learn:

- to use and adapt rules, strategies and tactics, using their knowledge of basic principles of attack and defence
- to develop the range and consistency of their skills, especially in specific net game

Extreme 'Keepy Uppies'

Resources – One ball and racket per child

Task – Holding the racket like a frying pan, children simply hit the ball in a controlled manner into the air and try to repeat this as many times as possible. As children grow in confidence the racket can be rotated or the edge and the handle of the racket can be used as well to bounce the ball upon.

Round and Round

Resources – One racket per child and one ball per group

Task – In teams of 6/8, standing in a line on either side of a net, children hit the ball co-operatively over and run to the back of their group. Players attempt to keep the rally going playing one shot each. As children get better they can run around to the back of the other team and play more competitively.

Pairs Volley

Resources – One racket per child and one ball per pair

Task – In pairs, children co-operatively try to volley the ball to each other without it touching the floor. A 'beat the clock' element could also be introduced as the children progress.

Different Strokes

Resources – One ball and racket per child

Task – Using a clear wall space, children attempt to hit alternate backhand and forehand strokes. Individually, emphasis should be placed on footwork and being in the right position to play the correct shot. Consideration must be given to safety if this is taught as a whole class activity.

FOCUS ACTIVITIES

Progression 1

In pairs, children co-operatively throw and catch a ball to each other. The ball should be thrown underarm mimicking the arm swing in tennis and should bounce once before being caught. By now children should be encouraged to throw and catch one handed and if extension is required, the less dominant hand only should be used.

Progression 2

The aim of the game is to score points by patting a ball underarm into the opponent's court area and making it bounce twice. Play the game one against one or two against two. Use a low net or bench to separate an area that will make a longer court area. Children should throw the ball in to serve and from then onwards hit or 'pat' the ball with their hand over the net – mimicking the action of a racket. Play up to 7 points before starting a new game. As well as continuing to develop greater control and learning more effective ways to win points, children should be encouraged to see the importance of footwork and getting quickly to where the ball is going to bounce.

Progression 3

The aim of the game is to score points by hitting a ball into your opponent's court and the ball bouncing twice. Play the game one against one on a long, narrow court using an appropriate racket and sponge ball. Children should serve underarm from behind the back of the court (or baseline). Players score a point when the ball lands in the court and bounces twice.

STRIKING & FIELDING GAMES

Presently, Striking and Fielding Games probably get most attention in the curriculum during the late spring and summer terms – when the weather is nicer. In many cases this will constitute splitting the class into large groups (sometimes in half) and playing huge games of cricket/rounders where pupils spend large periods of time either sitting down waiting to bat or standing waiting for a ball that never comes. What is more, when action does occur e.g. batting in rounders, the situation is either so difficult or inappropriate that the child often misses and experiences failure. These situations have no place in good PE practice and as teachers we must work harder to facilitate more effective experiences in striking and fielding games.

A key point that should be stressed again here, as can be seen from the summarised programmes of study outlined in the PE National Curriculum for Key Stages 1 and 2 shown below, is that the use of small sided and modified games is specified as a preferred mode of delivery.

Key Stage 1:

Pupils should be taught to:
a.   travel with, send and receive a ball and other equipment in different ways
b.   develop these skills for simple net, striking/fielding and invasion-type games
c.   play simple, competitive net, striking/fielding and invasion-type games that they and others have made, using simple tactics for attacking and defending.

Key Stage 2:

Pupils should be taught to:
a.   play and make up small-sided and modified competitive net, striking/fielding and invasion games
b.   use skills and tactics and apply basic principles suitable for attacking and defending
c.   work with others to organise and keep the games going.

The ideas here are focused upon cricket and rounders as a vehicle for this area, as it is possibly the area that Primary schools are best equipped to provide (though it is relatively easy to apply the same principles to other striking and fielding games). The lesson ideas provided are linked to the following QCA Schemes of work for Physical Education:

Year 1 & 2:	**(Unit 4) Games Activities 2**
Year 3 & 4:	**(Unit 12) Striking and Fielding Games 1**
Year 5 & 6:	**(Unit 25) Striking and Fielding Games 2**

KEY POINTS FOR IMPLEMENTATION

When delivering effective Striking and Fielding Games in Primary school there are three fundamental principles that need to be considered:

Develop activities that have high participation and action

Taking part in activities such as cricket and rounders often involve long periods of inactivity but during PE sessions it does not have to be this way. Be imaginative and create situations which mean that players rotate regularly or take part in other activities whilst they are waiting for a turn e.g. fielding practices for those next into bat.

Select and use appropriate equipment

Hard balls hurt, rubber balls bounce higher than you expect and small, thin, round faced rounders bats are very difficult to hit a moving ball with, especially if it doesn't bounce. These are universal truths about equipment yet we still persist in using all these items when the age or the ability of the child is less than appropriate. Using a wider range of resources is key to experiencing success in the principles of striking and fielding games so if we don't want pupils to miss the ball and walk to first base every time they bat, try giving them a tennis racket!

And again . . . . Remember to teach and not just manage

Consider a point made before but again so vital within striking and fielding games. It is easy to be satisfied once the children have been organised into teams to simply allow them to 'get on with it'. However, it is important to remember to keep teaching them rather than to simply manage the activity (a regular criticism from OFSTED). Opportunities can be found at many different times during a session to demonstrate or give specific teaching points and as natural breaks occur during striking and fielding games, there are ideal opportunities to stop or 'freeze' a game and ask questions such as 'Show me where you should try and hit the ball? Why?'

ACTIVITIES FOR YEARS 1 & 2

Children should learn:
- to improve the way they coordinate and control their bodies and a range of equipment
- to choose, use and vary simple tactics

Shooting Hoops

Resources – Multiple hoops, large bouncy balls

Task – Hoops are scattered randomly across a hard surface. In pairs, children move around the space and bounce the ball into the hoop, for their partner to catch. More able pupils can use tennis balls.

Gates

Resources – Pairs of markers, variety of balls

Task – Pairs of markers are scattered across a space to make a 'gate' (preferably colour coded). In pairs pupils find a gate and aim to roll the ball through it. Encourage children to be stationary before they throw to develop accuracy. This activity can be differentiated by using different sized balls and gates.

Bounce, Clap, Catch

Resources – One ball per child

Task – Various challenges of bouncing, throwing and catching can be set but one of the most useful involves asking children to bounce a ball, clap their hands and catch the ball. The more able the child, the more times they can try and clap their hands.

French Cricket

Resources – Foam balls only, variety of bats and rackets

Task – In pairs, a child tries to hit the legs of another with a foam ball. The batter tries to hit the ball away to prevent this from happening. Wherever the ball lands is where the ball should be bowled from so this will develop throwing over a variety of distances.

Slider

Resources – Beanbags, different coloured hoops

Task – Hoops are placed at varying distances away from the thrower. Children are encouraged to slide a beanbag along the floor so that it hits or lands in a hoop. Scores can be given if needed with higher scores for the hoops furthest away.

Strike!

Resources – Beanbags, large beach ball

Task – Two small teams (no more than 5) stand behind a line and face each other and aim beanbags at a beach ball so that it rolls away from them. The first team to knock the beach ball over their opponents' line is the winner.

Kick Rounders

Resources – 6 large balls, cones

Task – Four or five bases can be set out with cones. No bowlers are used. A batter or kicker in this case attempts to kick six balls one after the other and then run around the bases. The fielding team may not move until the kicker has finished. The fielding team must retrieve all six balls and place them in a hoop (where a bowler would stand) in order to stop the kicker scoring.

ACTIVITIES FOR YEARS 3 & 4

Children should learn:
- to consolidate and develop the range and consistency of their skills in striking and fielding games
- to choose and use a range of simple tactics and strategies
- to keep, adapt and make rules for striking and fielding games

Raiders

Resources – Hoops, beanbags

Task – A team of children (no more than 6) place a coloured hoop on the floor with colour coded beanbags inside the hoop. One child from each team then runs to anothers team's hoop, steals a beanbag and takes it back to their own hoop. The game can run for as long as required and multiple teams and hoops can be used but care must be taken not to bump heads when picking up beanbags!

Caterpillar Bounce

Resources – One ball per group of six

Task – In groups of six/eight, standing in two lines, children attempt to pass a ball from one line to another by throwing a ball under arm and bouncing once. Once a pass has been made the passer runs to the other end of the line ready to receive the ball again once it has zigzagged along. Competition can be added by racing caterpillars against each other.

Thread the Needle

Resources – Four cones and a ball (hoop optional)

Task – In pairs, bowl the ball underarm so that it bounces once and goes between two posts. Place a hoop on the ground at varying lengths to provide a focus. Points can be awarded for successful efforts and the game made harder as posts are narrowed. Also try using both left and right hands. Single cones can be aimed at for the most able.

Quick Cricket

Resources – One set of stumps, two cones, one marker, one bat, one ball

Task – An equilateral triangle of stumps and cones is set out. The bowler bowls from a marker towards the stumps. When the batter hits the ball they run around either cone and back to the stumps again. The ball is returned to the bowler and the process is repeated. This can also be made non stump and successful batters should retire when they reach a designated score e.g. 20.

Batting Lanes 1

Resources – One set of stumps, one bat, one ball, markers

Task – Children work here in small groups to practise their skills in a narrow strip of space. There is no bowler but instead the batter hits the ball off a tee or marker placed somewhere in front of the wickets. Two or three fielders are also added where appropriate; so three or four pupils can work together. Every three hits, players change positions. To make this more challenging underarm bowling can be added later. In addition batters could score points by hitting the ball over lines scoring 1, 2 or 3 depending on how far the ball goes.

Throwing Rounders

Resources – 3 tennis balls, cones

Task – Four or five bases can be set out with cones. No bowlers are used. A batter or thrower in this case attempts to throw three balls one after the other and then run around the bases. The fielding team must retrieve all three tennis balls and place them in a hoop (where a bowler would stand) in order to stop the thrower scoring.

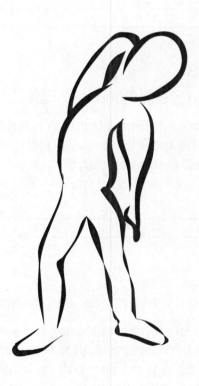

ACTIVITIES FOR YEARS 5 & 6

Children should learn:
- to develop the range and consistency of their skills, especially in specific striking and fielding games
- to use and adapt rules, strategies and tactics, using their knowledge of basic principles of batting and fielding

Catch Me If You Can

Resources – Tennis balls or beanbags

Task – In pairs, children experiment with a range of throws including low, high and side to side. On each occasion the partner must try to use the correct technique e.g. little fingers together for low 'scoop catch', thumbs and forefingers together for high catches.

Making a Barrier

Resources – Tennis balls

Task – In pairs, children roll the ball to each other. As the ball approaches them, the receiver should turn one of their knees inwards and place this next to their heel, thus making a barrier to stop the ball. Pick up the ball as normal and roll it back again. As children progress the ball can be rolled at either side of the receiver.

Fetch!

Resources – Tennis balls

Task – In pairs, one child rolls the ball while the other chases after it, picks it up and throws it back accurately to the roller. This can be repeated a few times before the pairs change over. This practice may seem simple but because it combines different elements of rolling, running, picking up, throwing and catching it can be quite demanding.

Pairs Cricket

Resources – Two sets of stumps, two bats and a ball, recording materials

Task – This game effectively looks like a 'proper' game of cricket but is broken down into pairs rather than teams – it is a great intermediate step. Children work in 5 or 6 pairs (Bowler & Wicket keeper, two batters, two or three pairs of fielders and an umpire and scorer). Each pair starts with 100 runs and loses 6 every time they are out. Runs are scored in the normal way by running and players rotate positions e.g. batters become fielders, fielders become bowler and wicket keeper etc. every two overs (or twelve balls).

Batting Lanes 2

Resources – One set of stumps, one bat, one ball, markers

Task – Children work here in small groups to practise their skills in a narrow strip of space. The bowler bowls to a batter defending their wickets. Behind the wickets is a wicket keeper. Two fielders are also added where appropriate; so five pupils can work together. Every six balls, players change positions. To make this more challenging bowlers should bowl over arm and batters score points by hitting the ball through gates (made by two markers) which can be placed in different positions in order to encourage certain shots.

Running Rounders

Resources – Flat bats, tennis balls, cones

Task – Four or five bases can be set out with cones. A bowler bowls to a batter with a flat bat who attempts to hit the ball and then run around the bases. However, to score a point the whole team must follow behind the batter. This game encourages lots of running and can be varied by moving the bases at different times.
N.B. This game does not necessarily have to exceed twelve children - multiple games can be occurring!

ATHLETICS

Athletics has been something of a neglected area of the PE National Curriculum due to reasons such as lack of training, a lack of resources and the fact that the present curriculum only requires it be taught in Key Stage 2 and allows schools the opportunity to drop it altogether if they so wish.

In some schools, Athletics will stil be allocated a reasonable share of curriculum time but unsurprisingly with constant pressure on school timetables, areas like Athletics which are considered optional, will continue to get pushed to one side.

Popularly, Athletics is delivered in most Primary schools in the summer term, culminating in an end of year sports day or school competition. In extreme cases it will be omitted completely and in odd situations, schools will justify that the core skills of running, jumping and throwing are covered adequately when delivering games such as netball and basketball.

However, there is a strong case to suggest that as running, jumping and throwing comprise core skills that permeate many other areas of the PE National Curriculum, dedicated time should be given to develop these skills to their optimum – namely through the teaching of Athletics.

In the interests of continuity and progression the development of provision for Athletics in Key Stage 1 should be encouraged which would underpin the programme of study outlined in the PE National Curriculum for Key Stage 2 shown below:

Pupils should be taught to:

a. take part in and design challenges and competitions that call for precision, speed, power or stamina
b. use running, jumping and throwing skills both singly and in combination
c. pace themselves in these challenges and competitions.

The lesson ideas provided are linked to the following QCA Schemes of work for Physical Education:

> **Year 1 & 2: (Unit 17) Athletic Activities 1**
>
> **Year 3 & 4: (Unit 18) Athletic Activities 2**
>
> **Year 5 & 6: (Unit 29) Athletic Activities 3**

KEY POINTS FOR IMPLEMENTATION

When delivering enjoyable and effective athletics in Primary school there are three fundamental principles that need to be considered:

Appropriateness of activity

As a result of the influence of our adult perspective of athletics, there is a very strong need to develop and modify activities to suit the children. For example, you may wish to concentrate on sprinting during a session or two but the recognised 'adult' distance of 100 metres is somewhat overtaxing for the majority of children – it will often turn into a stamina event rather than a speed event!

Don't focus on technique too early

When technique becomes the focus, it is often the case that children have insufficient strength or ability to copy advanced techniques correctly or use them to their advantage. The crouch start in sprinting being a case in point here, where children use most of their energy 'getting up,' rather than propelling themselves quickly forwards.

Develop pupils' understanding

By 'teaching for understanding' children will quickly gain an understanding of how the body moves which in turn provides a solid foundation for engaging in the fundamental athletic activities of running, jumping and throwing. In order to enable children to develop the required understanding, focused questioning and problem solving activities are a most effective tool e.g. 'What helps you run quickly?', 'Do you jump further/higher with your arms by your side?', 'When throwing, is it better to stand sideways or face forwards?'

It is hoped that as both teachers and children become used to this way of thinking that the posing and solving of questions/problems will become a regular occurrence not only within athletics lessons but within many other Physical Education lessons as well.

The ideas that follow include a range of both problem solving questions (PSQ) and activities based around running, jumping and throwing that can be used flexibly when delivering Athletics sessions.

ACTIVITIES FOR YEARS 1 & 2

Children should learn:

- to remember, repeat and link combinations of actions
- to use their bodies and a variety of equipment with greater control and coordination
- to choose skills and equipment to help them meet the challenges they are set
- to watch, copy and describe what they and others have done

RUNNING

Traffic Lights

Resources – None

Task – Children should find a space and on the command of 'GO', they must move/jog in the area provided, without making contact with anyone else. If the teacher calls out 'RED' the children should run on the spot. If the teacher calls out 'AMBER' the children should jog, carefully avoiding each other. If the teacher calls out 'GREEN' the children should run quickly and dodge each other, remembering to keep their head up!

Touching Base

Resources – Markers

Task – In a 10 x 20 metre area scatter a mixture of coloured markers (perhaps 10 of each colour). Set the PSQ of 'How many red markers can you touch/turn over in 30 seconds?' Extend activity by giving increasingly less time.

Slalom

Resources – Markers

Task – Design a zigzag course through which children have to run. Identify a path by using pairs of markers to make 'gates' through which children must pass. Keep gates 5 – 10 metres from each other to develop both speed and the changing of direction.

Fetch

Resources – Beanbags

Task – Lay out a line of bean bags at regular intervals, approximately 5 metres apart. Children are required to collect the nearest beanbag and bring it back to the line where they started. The next nearest should then be collected etc., with the furthest beanbag collected last this can be used individually, in pairs or in teams.

Shape Shifting

Resources – Markers

Task – In the space available, lay out yellow markers to make circlular patterns, red markers to make square patterns and blue markers to make triangular patterns. In three lines or snakes, children can follow their leader around different pathways by following different coloured markers.

JUMPING

Caterpillar Jump

Resources – Hoops (barriers optional)

Task – Lay a wavy line (or caterpillar) of hoops on the ground. In pairs, children can follow the caterpillar by either hopping from hoop to hoop or jumping from two feet to two feet. Extension can be provided by either performing alternating hops or two footed jumps or by adding barriers between hoops.

Crossing The Stream

Resources – Ropes

Task – Mark out an ever widening stream on the ground using skipping ropes. Children are encouraged to challenge themselves to jump over the stream at the widest part they are able. **N.B.** Jumps should take off from one foot and land on two feet, bending knees on landing.

Hopper

Resources – Markers

Task – Mark out a 10 metre square with markers. Children should hop down one side of the square, jog down the second side, hop on the other foot down the third side and jog down the last side. The reason for breaking up the hopping is so not to place too much stress on the ankle.

Jumping PSQs

Resources – Optional

Task – Solve the following problems (ideally children should work in pairs).
Can you jump across the space (e.g. a badminton court) in less than five jumps?
How many hops does it take to cover 10 metres?
Can you jump further than the distance between your head and your feet when you are lying down? How many hand spans can you jump?
Working in pairs, estimate and measure.

Shooting Hoops

Resources – Hoops, beanbags

Task – Lay out a random pattern of coloured hoops in a 10 x 10 metre space. Standing in a hoop in the middle of the space, children must attempt to throw a beanbag of a corresponding colour into each hoop.

Throwing PSQs

Resources – Beanbags, range of balls

Task – Solve the following problems (ideally children should work in pairs)
Can you throw further than you can run in three seconds or jump in five jumps?
Can you throw a small ball higher than the mark on the wall?
How far can you throw a large ball with two hands?
Estimate and measure using steps.

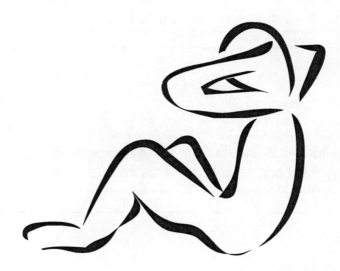

ACTIVITIES FOR YEARS 3 & 4

Children should learn:
- to consolidate and improve the quality, range and consistency of the techniques they use for particular activities
- to develop their ability to choose and use simple tactics and strategies in different situations
- to describe and evaluate the effectiveness of performances, and recognise aspects of performances that need improving

RUNNING

Shared Relay

Resources – Relay batons or beanbags

Task – In teams of four, find out either the best way of running the fastest time as a relay team over a shared distance of 60m or the longest distance as a relay team over times of 1 minute.
N.B. This may mean different members of the team running different distances.

Compass Run

Resources – 5 markers

Task – Arrange markers to represent the points of a compass (N, E, S, W) with the fifth marker placed in the centre. The distance from the centre marker to each compass point should be between 5 and 10 metres. On the command of 'GO' children should run from the centre marker to each compass point in turn. After visiting a compass point a return journey should be made to the centre each time.

Shuttle Run

Resources – 2 markers

Task – Mark a distance of approx. 10 metres between two points (A and B). Children should then sprint as fast as possible from point A to point B. Upon reaching point B children should turn quickly and return to A. This can be repeated for 4 to 6 'shuttles'.

Low Hurdles

Resources – Hurdles/barriers

Task – Mark out a distance of approx. 20 metres and every 3 to 4 metres place a low barrier (30cm high approx.) Ideally, purpose made plastic hurdles would be used but if not a barrier can be made by placing a cane or rope over two cones. Children should be encouraged to run quickly over the hurdles and NOT jump. Ask questions such as, *'Are you faster if you take off from one foot or two? Why? Is it better to hurdle with the same leg each time?'*

JUMPING

Standing Long Jump

Resources – Beanbags

Task – Children should try and jump as far as they can from a standing position. Encourage children to bend their knees and swing their arms whilst 'looking ahead' to where they might land. Children can work in pairs and mark each jump with a beanbag.

Spring Jumps

Resources – Beanbags

Task – As above but try and link 3 - 5 jumps together without stopping.

Combination Jumping

Resources – Different coloured hoops

Task – Children should be encouraged to jump from one hoop to another, using different combinations of feet e.g. take off from one foot and land on two feet. Challenges can be varied by giving different rules to different colours e.g. all red hoops are take off and land on two feet.

Jumping PSQs

Resources – Optional

Task – Solve the following problems (ideally children should work in pairs)
How do your arms effect how high/far you jump? What happens if you put your hands on your head, let your arms swing or put them behind your back?

THROWING

Target Practice

Resources – Hoops and various objects to throw

Task – Position hoops at distances up to 20 metres away and challenge the children to accurately throw objects into them whilst standing behind a line. Different throws and objects can be used to extend the activity e.g. throw a beanbag underarm, throw a tennis ball over arm, throw a large ball with two hands and sling a quoit.

It's Over My Head

Resources – Large balls

Task – Children face each other in pairs. One child attempts to throw a large ball using a two handed throw over the other child's head. From wherever the ball lands the other child attempts to throw the ball back over the first child's head. This encourages children to throw 'high' rather than 'flat'.

Throwing PSQs

Resources – Beanbags, range of balls

Task – Solve the following problems (ideally children should work in pairs)
Can you throw further with one hand or two? Under arm or over arm? Try with a range of objects (beanbags, small and large balls etc.)
Do people with longer arms throw furthest?

ACTIVITIES FOR YEARS 5 & 6

Children should learn:
- to develop the consistency of their actions in a number of events
- to increase the number of techniques they use
- to choose appropriate techniques for specific events
- to evaluate their own and others' work and suggest ways to improve it

RUNNING

Record Breakers

Resources – None

Task – Set the challenge of breaking an individual world record by using a team approach e.g. 'Can your team run faster than the 800 metres world record?' (approx. 1 min. 41 secs.), 'How many people is it best to have in the team?', 'How far should each person run?'

Paired Relay

Resources – Relay batons

Task – Identify a circular course of approx. 200 metres. Children work in pairs to complete the course. Child A leaves from the start line carrying a baton whilst Child B leaves from the finish line. At a point during the course they should meet and when this occurs they exchange the baton. Child A runs back to the start line whilst Child B runs to the finish line with the baton. The winning pair is the first to cross their respective lines.

Pass It On

Resources – Large balls

Task – Children form teams of 5/8 members and stand one behind the other, with the last member holding a large ball. On the command 'GO' the team jogs to a predetermined point. As the team are moving, the last member sprints to the front of the line and then passes the ball backwards which is then passed backwards through the line. The process is repeated each time the ball arrives at the back and continues until the finishing point is reached.

Quick Change

Resources – Relay batons

Task – In pairs, children experiment with different ways of how to change a relay baton quickly. Pairs should start with one of the pair running towards another and then progress with one of the pair running up behind.
N.B. Encourage children to spread their thumb and index finger (make a large 'V') ready to receive the baton but to also keep their fingers together to avoid injury.

Running PSQs

Resources – None

Task – Solve the following problems (ideally children should work in pairs)
How far can you run in: 5 seconds, 30 seconds, 2 minutes?
Estimate and measure accurately. Try and set your own targets for improvement.

JUMPING

Five Step Long Jump

Resources – Beanbags

Task – Using a run up of only 5 steps (any small odd number will do) children should try and jump as far as they can from behind a line. The important aspect here is to encourage children to get faster as they approach the take off and not to slow (or look) down. Children can work in pairs and mark each start position and jump with a beanbag. If a child under steps the line simply move the beanbag back and if they over step, move the beanbag forward. As before, encourage children to bend their knees on landing.

Hooped Triple Jump

Resources – Hoops

Task – The basic footwork of the triple jump can be learned working 'backwards' using hoops. Firstly, repeat the above activity but place the take off foot in a hoop, rather than use a line. Secondly, place a second hoop next to the first and encourage the children to place their other foot in this hoop before reaching the take off hoop. Thirdly, the foot that was placed in the second hoop should also be placed in this hoop. A footwork pattern should now emerge of either Left – Left – Right and land on two feet or Right – Right – Left and land on two feet. As the children become more proficient the gaps between the hoops can be widened. It is advised that this activity be done on grass as it means the hoops do not slide and that the ground provides more cushioning.

Scissor Jumping

Resources – Cones, canes or ropes

Task – Make a barrier by placing a cane or rope over two cones. Children can begin by standing sideways on to the barrier and stepping over it, closest leg first and then the leg furthest away. As confidence grows speed up the process and add a run up that follows a curved pathway up to the barrier. The same approach to marking out a five step run up by using a beanbag can be followed from the long jump section above.

THROWING

Throwing PSQs

Resources – Beanbags, small balls, quoits

Task – Solve the following problems (ideally children should work in pairs)
Do you throw further with a run-up or without? Try using different equipment, e.g. hoops, large and small balls, quoits, beanbags.
Is it better to face the way you are throwing or stand sideways on?
How do your legs help when throwing?
How far can you throw if you cannot use your legs?
Throw whilst sitting or kneeling. Compare to standing throw.
Does throwing with your weaker hand improve with repeated attempts?

N.B. Key teaching points to convey here are:
*   Throw the object from low to high
*   Throw the object as fast as possible
*   Ensure the object is the last thing that moves forward (it is especially important to keep the elbow ahead of the object for as long as possible)
*   Create a 'safety line' which no one crosses until permission is given

GYMNASTICS

Gymnastics, like both Dance and Games is central to all long term PE planning in Primary schools. Like Dance, it allows the ability to demonstrate very specific body control and to focus upon high quality movement. However, despite the amount of time allowed for Gymnastics in most schools, the quality produced by those at the end of Key Stage 2 is not always as advanced as it might be.

In order to maximise the potential of this activity area, clear progression must be identified across the year groups, which includes more advanced movements and application on different apparatus.

As a structure, the PE National Curriculum of course offers nothing more than a starting point:

Key Stage 1

Pupils should be taught to:
a.   perform basic skills in travelling, being still, finding space and using it safely, both on the floor and using apparatus
b.   develop the range of their skills and actions (for example, balancing, taking off and landing, turning and rolling)
c.   choose and link skills and actions in short movement phrases
d.   create and perform short, linked sequences that show a clear beginning, middle and end and have contrasts in direction, level and speed.

Key Stage 2

Pupils should be taught to:
a.   create and perform fluent sequences on the floor and using apparatus
b.   include variations in level, speed and direction in their sequences.

The lesson ideas provided are linked to the following QCA Schemes of work for Physical Education:

> **Year 1 & 2:   (Unit 5 & 6) Gymnastic Activities 1 & 2**
>
> **Year 3 & 4:   (Unit 14 & 15) Gymnastic Activities 3 & 4**
>
> **Year 5 & 6:   (Unit 27 & 28) Gymnastic Activities 5 & 6**

KEY POINTS FOR IMPLEMENTATION

When delivering effective Gymnastics in Primary school there are three fundamental principles that need to be considered:

Progression

When much of what is expected in each year group is a 'sequence of movements' it is very easy to either repeat what has been taught in early years, or simply not move on enough. To maximise the time available and the potential of each child, it is important to have a clear plan of what should be taught and when, across the school. Such progression should not only include specific movements (travels, balances and rolls etc.) but should also include how and when such movements are performed (on small/large apparatus).

Extend onto apparatus

Many Primary schools are blessed with a variety of basic gymnastic equipment, including frames that are rarely, if ever used – often just forming an attractive wall decoration in the dinner hall! Though such equipment can look daunting, once basic instruction is given, it is very easy to position safely. The reason that such resources are so important, as indicated above, is that they develop an essential progression of movement from floor work.

N.B. Equipment is to be used and not something to be sat on when listening to instructions – this includes mats!

Quality of Movement

A feature of gymnastics when performed poorly is that movements are simply executed – a roll, a balance, a travel. This accepts that simply doing the activity is enough – which it is not. Focusing upon quality of movement should be a key feature of all Gymnastic lessons (just like Dance) and children should be shown, encouraged and corrected when necessary, to develop a sequence that 'looks good'. An area that should be given specific attention here is how movements are linked together. Links should be smooth and flow freely from one movement to another.

ACTIVITIES FOR YEAR 1 & 2

Children should learn:
- to move confidently and safely in their own and general space, using changes of speed, level and direction
- to copy or create and link movement phrases with beginnings, middles and ends
- to perform movement phrases using a range of body actions and body parts
- to remember, repeat and link combinations of gymnastic actions, body shapes and balances with control and precision

SHORT ACTIVITIES

Islands

Resources – Mats

Task – Children work on a specific mat (island) which has different rules/laws to other islands. When on an island these rules have to be obeyed. The idea is that children can be directed to perform a specific type of movement e.g. travel, but will have to do it according to their individual rules e.g. low, slowly, high. Rules can also be added to move (or swim!) from one island to another.

Copy Cats

Resources – Optional

Task – Ideas can be taken from above or the later extended tasks. The key idea is that in pairs, one child teaches another a short sequence of movements and the other child has to copy it. Such an activity is vital to develop the focus of evaluation and improvement. Conversation and time to practise are vital here too and performance should be encouraged wherever possible.

Opposites

Resources – Optional

Task – Ideas can be taken from above or the later extended tasks. Essentially this task is something of a progression from 'Copy Cats'. The key idea is that in pairs, one child teaches another a short sequence of movements and the other child has to produce a sequence that is opposite in nature e.g. if child 'A' goes high, child 'B' may go low. Such an activity develops thinking skills and encourages movement vocabulary, as children should articulate what they have done and why.

FOCUS ACTIVITIES

Progression 1

Choose different ways of travelling e.g. sidestepping and a basic roll; and link these to make a short movement phrase which can be repeated and performed on the floor. Encourage the children to explore different shapes that can be made at the start and finish.

Progression 2

Choose three 'like' actions e.g. *three different jumps* or *three balances,* and link these actions to make a short movement phrase on the floor and/or apparatus. Take the opportunity to share movements with a partner, small group or the whole class.

Progression 3

Create and perform a simple sequence, on the floor and using mats, of up to four elements, e.g. balance, roll, jump, shape. Make sure children show a clear starting position and that they move smoothly between shapes and actions. Comments should focus upon specific qualities shown.

Progression 4

Encourage children to transfer sequences so that they use a combination of floor, mats and apparatus, e.g. move from the floor to finish on apparatus, or move from apparatus to finish on the floor.

ACTIVITIES FOR YEAR 3 & 4

Children should learn:
- to consolidate and improve the quality of their actions, body shapes and balances, and their ability to link phrases of movement
- to develop the range of actions, body shapes and balances they include in a performance
- to create gymnastic sequences that meet a theme or set of conditions
- to use compositional devices when creating their sequences, such as changes in speed, level and direction

SHORT ACTIVITIES

Double Act

Resources – Various

Task – In pairs, children devise a short sequence that can focus upon words such as 'contrast' or 'matching'. Pairs would be expected to perform together and should be encouraged to focus here not only upon the quality of their movements but also their timing.

Playback

Resources – Various

Task – Ideas can be taken from above or the later extended tasks. Children can work individually or again in pairs. Once a basic sequence has been devised, the children are instructed to imagine that the teacher has pressed a button on their video machine. This can be either 'play', 'fast forward', 'rewind' or 'pause'. Such a task will present the children with a mix of problems to solve that will extend and challenge all.

Fundamental Skills 1 – Forward and Backward Rolls

Resources – Mats

Task – Forward Rolls
Starting from a crouch position, children should put their hands down, shoulder width apart. Keeping chin tucked, and pushing through with the legs, children should complete a forward roll. Remember to have feet tucked under the bottom to enable standing up.

N.B. A good tip to close the body shape during rolls is to place a beanbag either under the chin (to tuck in the head and round the shoulders) or between the knees.

Task – Backward Rolls
Start from crouch position, children should put their hands up by the ears. Sitting and quickly rolling backwards, the aim is to get the hands touching the floor. As this occurs, lift the bottom and push with the hands and complete the roll to standing.

FOCUS ACTIVITIES

Progression 1

Ask children to create and perform a sequence of contrasting actions that uses both floor and apparatus e.g. three jumps and two balances, which shows contrasting shapes. Make sure children show maximum extension when balancing and flow easily when transferring weight, so that the end of one action is the beginning of another.

Progression 2

Using floor and mats, ask children to create and perform a sequence that involves a clear change of speed and links pairs of multiple actions together in different ways e.g. three rolls and three balances.

Progression 3

Ask children to create a sequence using both floor and mats that has six different elements e.g. body shape, travel, roll, balance, jump, weight on hands. Basic graphical notation could be encouraged here, so that children can remember what they have done both during the session and from week to week.

Progression 4

Children should explore ways in which the sequence they have devised above could be linked with another. Ideally, children should find at least one way of coming together. Opportunities should also be found to extend this on apparatus.

ACTIVITIES FOR YEAR 5 & 6

Children should learn:

- to select, combine and perform skills, actions and balances, including some that are inverted
- to develop their own gymnastic sequences by understanding, choosing and applying a range of compositional principles

SHORT ACTIVITIES

Group Time

Resources – Optional

Task – In small groups, children devise a short sequence that explores and develops different 'timings' e.g. canon, unison, mirrored, synchronised. This is a great opportunity to bring together, thoughts, ideas, notation, performance, evaluation and improvement.

Up!

Resources – Various apparatus

Task – As well as having the opportunity to devise a sequence on apparatus, it is important that they have the opportunity to experience some sense of 'flight' off it. Though this may develop naturally or with a structured question, a controlled experience can also be devised. This can be as simple as children travelling along a bench, jumping off the end and landing safely. More complex movements such as turns and shapes in the air can be added as children progress.

Fundamental Skills 2 – Headstand/Handstand/Cartwheel

Resources – Mats

Task – Headstand
From a kneeling position, children should make a triangle on the floor with head and hands. Placing the front of the top of the head on the floor, walk the feet in tiny steps towards the hands. As more weight comes onto the head and hands try and lift the feet off the floor. Keep the knees tucked into the chest.

Task – Handstand
Children should place hands on the floor shoulder width apart and gain confidence with kicking legs into the air before landing back on their feet again. With support (a person or a wall) children should be encouraged to flick one leg higher until it is pointing upwards, with the other shortly following, ankles together. Encourage children to look back through their hands, so to straighten the body.

Task – Cartwheel
Children should place hands on the floor shoulder width apart and gain confidence with bunny hopping legs over a hoop or line. Encourage the kicking of legs higher and wider and focus upon the placing of foot – hand – hand – foot. Finally straighten out by performing this around an arc and then along a line.

FOCUS ACTIVITIES

Progression 1

Using both floor and mats, ask children to work with a partner or in a small group to create and perform a gymnastic sequence of at least eight elements. The sequence should include changes of direction and level, and incorporate different shapes and balances. If possible, different timings learned in the short activities could also be added.

Progression 2

Ask children to modify the above sequence, so that it can be performed on apparatus. For further challenge, encourage the children to explore moving from apparatus, to floor and back to apparatus again.

Progression 3

Ask children to compose, notate and perform a sequence that has ten different elements. Ideally it should include twisting and turning, basic flight, changes of direction and speed, and contrasting shapes and balances.

Progression 4

Ask children to adapt the sequence created above so that it can be performed in a small group, using the floor and apparatus. Different timings learned in the short activities should be evident.

DANCE

Though Dance always gets plenty of attention in Primary schools and is central to nearly all long term PE planning, the delivery itself can often 'leave a lot to be desired'. For instance, in some schools, lessons can still take the form of the teacher pressing 'play' on the tape recorder and following the thirty minute Dance tape.

Dance deserves better than this and taught well, represents features of Physical Education that should be held most dear; the ability to demonstrate very specific body control and to focus upon high quality movement. To this end it is important that schools plan interesting and challenging activities and support their staff in being able to implement the curriculum effectively.

As a structure, the PE National Curriculum of course offers nothing more than a starting point:

Key Stage 1

Pupils should be taught to:
a. use movement imaginatively, responding to stimuli, including music, and perform basic skills (for example, travelling, being still, making a shape, jumping, turning and gesturing)
b. change the rhythm, speed, level and direction of their movements
c. create and perform dances using simple movement patterns, including those from different times and cultures
d. express and communicate ideas and feelings.

Key Stage 2

Pupils should be taught to:
a. create and perform dances using a range of movement patterns, including those from different times, places and cultures
b. respond to a range of stimuli and accompaniment.

The lesson ideas provided are linked to the following QCA Schemes of work for Physical Education:

> **Year 1 & 2: (Unit 1 & 2) Dance Activities 1 & 2**
>
> **Year 3 & 4: (Unit 8 & 9) Dance Activities 3 & 4**
>
> **Year 5 & 6: (Unit 21 & 22) Dance Activities 5 & 6**

KEY POINTS FOR IMPLEMENTATION

When delivering effective Dance in Primary school, three fundamental principles appear to 'leap out'.

Capture the imagination of the children

Using music that both you and your class can relate to is always a good start. It encourages both interest and the desire for movement. In addition, if children are encouraged to count (in fours or eights) then it also helps to develop the concept of moving in time. To create a sense of ownership for Dance, it is important to find opportunities to let the children develop their own ideas, though this is often best achieved within a structure e.g. individual work follows a piece that everybody has been taught and performs together. Most importantly of all, an opportunity should be found for a class to perform their work – whether it be to another class, the whole school or at a festival. This not only encourages both the teacher and the children to produce quality work as all are on public display but essentially it gives the activity a reason for being.

Maintain focus upon quality of movement

A feature of Dance when performed poorly is that it is simply 'marked' through. This accepts that simply doing the activity is enough – which it is not. Focusing upon quality of movement should be a key feature of all Dance lessons and children should be shown, encouraged and corrected when necessary, to develop a sequence that 'looks good'. An area that should be given specific attention here is how movements are linked together. Links should be smooth and flow freely from one movement to another.

Use space intelligently

For reasons never quite understood, new groups of both children and undergraduates will often begin performing movements whilst going around in a big circle (usually clockwise). Dance above all other areas of the PE curriculum provides a perfect opportunity to teach a class about how best to use space both in the area immediately around themselves and to develop an awareness of pathways across a large area. To this end, movement should never be produced without reason or purpose.

In addition to the usual activities found in other activity areas, focused activities have also been included to demonstrate examples of appropriate progressions required as the children move through the school.

ACTIVITIES FOR YEARS 1 & 2

Children should learn:

- to move confidently and safely in their own and general space, using changes of speed, level and direction
- to compose and link movement phrases to make simple dances with clear beginnings, middles and ends
- to perform movement phrases using a range of body actions and body parts
- to compose and perform dance phrases and short dances that express and communicate moods, ideas and feelings, choosing and varying simple compositional ideas
- to explore, remember, repeat and link a range of actions with coordination, control, and an awareness of the expressive qualities of the dance
- to watch and describe dance phrases and dances, and use what they learn to improve their own work

Toy Shop

Resources – A range of stimuli including words, pictures and objects

Task – Focus on the different ways that toys move e.g. a jack in a box suddenly 'springs up' or a rubber ball bounces along before it stops. Teach children actions to follow as an example. Ask the class to respond with different actions of their own, thinking of the stimuli used.

Follow the Birdie!

Resources – None

Task – In small groups (maximum 4) the leader of the group travels around the space mimicking the movement of birds e.g. flapping, gliding, swooping while the others follow.

In The Mood

Resources – Musical instruments

Task – Play a small selection of instruments e.g. tambourine, drum. Ask children to think about how each one makes them feel and then see if they can compose movements that will represent the music.

Statues

Resources – Tambourine

Task – Ask children to find an interesting position. When the tambourine is shaken they have to move/travel using key words e.g. heavy, quietly, quickly. When the tambourine is banged they should freeze, like statues in another interesting shape. Emphasise quality of movement here and select pupils to demonstrate.

FOCUS ACTIVITIES

Music here is optional but will develop the idea that Dance is performed with it - any music will do that will represent the seasons because timing isn't going to be important.

Step 1 – Use stimuli for summer. Consider pictures e.g. sun, travel brochures, words e.g. bright, happy and objects e.g. bucket and spade. Encourage each child to travel across the space and move in a way that conveys the mood of the season. Ideas are key here, so find time to share and watch each other move. Also, encourage children to identify qualities that they like in each other's work.

Step 2 – Repeat step 1 but work towards a set of movements for the contrasting season of winter. Again the more ideas and stimuli the better.

Step 3 – Let the children see if they change from summer into winter. This maybe difficult at first but take the time here. One possible way is to see if the children can help each other e.g. how can they get from one position to another? If the principle of linking movements is started early it will help enormously as the children get older.

Step 4 – Develop on one more step and let the children move from summer to winter and back to summer again. Allow others to watch and see if they can spot when the changes occur and how they know. Using appropriate vocabulary (see QCA scheme for list) should also be encouraged during comments.

Step 5 – If extension work is needed another season could be chosen. If this is the case, perhaps a small group could work together for autumn or spring.

ACTIVITIES FOR YEARS 3 & 4

Children should learn:
- to create and link dance phrases using a simple dance structure or motif
- to perform dances with an awareness of rhythmic, dynamic and expressive qualities, on their own, with a partner and in small groups
- to explore and create characters and narratives in response to a range of stimuli
- to use simple choreographic principles to create motifs and narrative
- to perform more complex dance phrases and dances that communicate character and narrative
- to describe and evaluate some of the compositional features of dances performed with a partner and in a group
- to talk about how they might improve their dances

Circus Performers

Resources – Brainstorm

Task – In the classroom, brainstorm words related to the circus. In the lesson have these words on display and encourage the children to try and move/behave like a particular character. If time allows, encourage the children to guess each others.

Animal Crackers

Resources – Music e.g. The Carnival

Task – Identify music that represents the quality of animals. See if the children can guess the animals and can compose movements that would represent them.

Movie Star

Resources – DVD or TV recordings

Task – Play sections of incidental music for film or TV and see if the children can guess what might be going on e.g. somebody creeping, scary, etc. Ask them to recreate the emotion or the action, without seeing the actual pictures.

Magic Mirror

Resources – None

Task – To encourage close watching and fine motor control, ask children to start by sitting opposite a partner. One child starts and slowly begins to move e.g. stretches up arm and the other tries to follow them exactly.

FOCUS ACTIVITY

Try and find some basic music that repeats e.g. 'popcorn' or 'variations'. The theme for this will be machines, that just go on and on, so music that has a strong repeated beat is ideal.

Step 1 – Ask children to explore what movements a machine or robot might make. Consider speed and direction e.g. a slow turning machine, moving up and down faster and faster. Make the movement last for a count of 8.

Step 2 – In pairs, teach partners a set of movements, so that both are able to repeat each others'. Ask pairs to practise linking both movements together e.g. one after the other, in unison. Pairs should perform at an early stage for the whole class.

Step 3 – Two pairs join together to become four. As a four the group should decide what kind of machine they wish to be. Encourage them to experiment how to work/move together. If this proves difficult children can work in two pairs within the group. Ideally, the group should develop a machinelike movement over two lots of 8, so encourage children to count aloud to begin with.

Step 4 – Return to the start now and teach a basic phrase that everyone can copy e.g. pretend to lift something up and then down and then side to side. This should be mechanical and very repetitive. Firstly, it sets the scene for the piece but secondly it allows those who find co-ordination difficult to follow movements and get a feel for the timing.

Step 5 – Start with step 4 and join on step 1 and 2. This will need lots of repetition. It should convey that the machine works well together and then breaks down by doing its own thing. The focus here should be given to the links between the sections.

Step 6 – Another step with lots of repetition. Repeat step 5 as a reminder and then try and join on their group work. This time the focus should be on quality of movement. Don't despair if the quality goes down initially. Each time a new section is added this will occur. However, practice will make things better!

ACTIVITIES FOR YEARS 5 & 6

Children should learn:
* to compose dances by using, adapting and developing steps, formations and patterning from different dance styles
* to perform dances expressively, using a range of performance skills
* to explore, improvise and combine movement ideas fluently and effectively
* to create and structure motifs, phrases, sections and whole dances
* to begin to use basic compositional principles when creating their dances
* to understand how a dance is formed and performed
* to describe, analyse, interpret and evaluate dances, showing an understanding of some aspects of style and context
* to evaluate, refine and develop their own and others' work

Eat Up!

Resources – None

Task – To enable children to develop fine motor control during movement ask children to mime eating bananas, ice creams and toffee apples. Make sure they take their time and mimic each tiny movement.

Lindy Hop

Resources – Link to 1920s and 1930s History

Task – This basic 1920s craze can be used to co-ordinate quick steps or as a motif. Simply kick one leg, double kick on the other leg, rock onto your front foot, onto your back foot and onto your front foot again. Repeat as many times and in as many directions as you require.

Collapse!

Resources – None

Task – Stretch up high and then imagine each body part, from the top down is magnetic. Collapse the body down and 'stick' each body part to another as you go down.

Copy Cats

Resources – None

Task – Each child composes a short dance phrase. They must then pair up on command and try to copy each other's work. Keep mixing the partners to focus their attention.

FOCUS ACTIVITIES

If possible try and choreograph a dance to a popular piece of music that many of the class will like. Ideally this should have a strong beat and it should be relatively easy to distinguish a count of 8.

Step 1 – Demonstrate a starting position and teach the class a basic step sequence of your choice that covers 2 lots of 8. Repeat if more time needs to be covered.

Step 2 – Give a basic structure e.g. travel, turn, travel, jump which they have to fill two lots of 8 with themselves. Allow plenty of time to practise and split the class regularly to allow one half to watch the other and make comment. The concept of pathways becomes important here too as they all need to consider exactly where they are travelling, so movements can be repeated.

Step 3 – Join step 1 and 2 together - remember quality is the key but it takes time. Try and get the music on early and allow them to practise with it. If timing proves difficult, allow the children to sit and listen to the music encouraging them to count and tap along to it. Get this step as good as possible before moving on.

Step 4 – In small groups (maximum of 6) encourage children to compose a group motif that covers two or four lots of 8. Differentiation can be brought in here as more able children can develop more complex sequences, whilst others may just wish to repeat. Encourage each group to consider what relationships they might choose e.g. lines, circle, unison, canon, partners. Again, experiment, practise and perform.

Step 5 – Step 3 and 4 now need joining which may prove initially messy as the individuals must find how to get into groups. Two possible solutions here. Firstly, children could change their pathways in step 2 so that they finish up with the rest of their group. Secondly, an extra count or two, of 8 can be used to allow travelling time between individual and group work.

Step 6 – Get each group to adapt their motif so that they can travel to a fixed location, e.g. a named child standing in the middle of the room. In turn each group travels to the location and freezes upon arrival. Allow each group a count of 8 to make the journey.

Step 7 – Finale! Lots of choices now. Either strike a dramatic finishing pose or if you need to extend the group further you could find a way back to either the group or individual work.

SWIMMING & WATER SAFETY

Next to Outdoor and Adventurous Activities (OAA), swimming is the next most neglected area of the PE National Curriculum. The reasons for the neglect are consistent with that of OAA but in this case, locating adequate facilities, pressure upon curriculum time and prohibitive costs must also be factored in. As a result, an increasing number of schools are electing not to take pupils swimming.

For many, however, learning to swim and gain confidence in water is one of the most important life skills that can be learned and so most schools still endeavour to make provision one way or another. The most popular way to offer swimming is to cater for it in one or two year groups only e.g. Years 3 and 4 and to send children to the nearest suitable pool where they are taught by swimming instructors.

In the interests of continuity and progression, however, a more desirable idea would be to develop provision of Swimming through both Key Stage 1 and 2 following the programme of study outlined in the PE National Curriculum shown below:

Key Stage 1

Pupils should be taught to:
a.   move in water (for example, jump, walk, hop and spin, using swimming aids and support)
b.   float and move with and without swimming aids
c.   feel the buoyancy and support of water and swimming aids
d.   propel themselves in water using different swimming aids, arm and leg actions and basic strokes.

Key Stage 2

Pupils should be taught to:
a.   pace themselves in floating and swimming challenges related to speed, distance and personal survival
b.   swim unaided for a sustained period of time over a distance of at least 25m
c.   use recognised arm and leg actions, lying on their front and back
d.   use a range of recognised strokes and personal survival skills (for example, front crawl, back crawl, breaststroke, sculling, floating and surface diving).

The lesson ideas provided are linked to the following QCA Schemes of work for Physical Education:

Year 1 & 2:   (Unit 7) Swimming Activities and Water Safety 1

Year 3, 4, 5 & 6: (Unit 16) Swimming Activities and Water Safety 2

KEY POINTS FOR IMPLEMENTATION

When delivering enjoyable and effective swimming for Primary aged children there are three fundamental principles that need to be considered:

Prioritise the development of water confidence

Like no other aspect of the PE curriculum, swimming has the capability of making children feel fearful because of the presence of water. Such behaviour is learned but on occasions, is so deeply rooted that it can present a real challenge to even the most effective teacher. While there is no sure way of overcoming such reactions, gaining water confidence at the earliest age possible is clearly desirable. As well as making the activities as fun as possible, this also requires the teacher to think hard about what the correct progression should be for any given child.

Use swimming aids and support intelligently

When children have yet to master a particular skill in water the obvious reaction is to provide the child with some kind of buoyancy aid whether it be armbands, floats or woggles. Though this clearly makes sense, it is important to see such resources only as tools to facilitate progression and differentiation, as children can become dependent on their use.

Differentiate, differentiate, differentiate!

When observing children closely in PE, nothing seems to separate children more in terms of ability than swimming. Though some instructors would classify groups into beginners, emerging swimmers and advanced for ease of management, the differences within such groups can be massive. Therefore it is vitally important that the teacher has a sound grasp of the different stages of development that each child needs to progress through to ensure that an appropriate challenge is set for each child.

In addition to the usual activities found in other activity areas, focused activities have also been included to demonstrate the appropriate progressions required as the children move through the school.

ACTIVITIES FOR YEARS 1 & 2

Children should learn:
- to work with confidence
- to explore and use skills, actions and ideas individually and in combination
- how to choose and use skills for different swimming tasks
- to improve the control and coordination of their bodies in water

SHORT ACTIVITIES

Bob

Resources – None

Task – Ask children to hold on to the side and bounce up and down in the water. Each time, try and make the challenges more difficult e.g. Can you put your shoulders under the water? Can you put your face in the water? Can you touch your ankle? As confidence increases, try activities in the open water.

Simon Says

Resources – None

Task – Call out different instructions for children to follow. Only when the instruction begins with Simon Says should they actually do what is asked. This activity allows the teacher to gauge water confidence as the amount of challenge is increased.

Follow My Leader

Resources – None

Task – In pairs or small groups, ask one child to move around the pool and ask others to follow their actions. Encourage leaders to move in different directions such as forwards, backwards and sideways, as well as using different movements.

The Bean Game

Resources – None

Task – The children are asked to make different body shapes depending on what type of bean the teacher calls out. e.g. String bean = long, tall shape, Baked bean = small, round shape, runner bean = run on the spot.

FOCUS ACTIVITIES

Progression 1

Begin with working on front crawl and start with legs first. Initially this can be done by holding onto the side. Follow this by supporting the body whilst swimming with a float under each arm, before moving on to the holding of one float out in front. Activities should also focus upon keeping a flat body position in the water. Finally, children can attempt to glide across and kick with legs unaided.

Progression 2

Once confidence has been developed with the above activities, attention can focus upon front crawl arms. This can be demonstrated and practised by the children by first holding onto the side. This time, one float only is to be used under one arm whilst a child propels themselves through the water using legs and one arm. Different conditions of arm and leg use can be set to provide different challenges.

Progression 3

Next, work can begin on back crawl and again start with legs first. Initially this can be done by holding onto the side. Follow this by supporting the body whilst swimming with a float under each arm, before moving on to the holding of one float over the chest. Activities should also focus on keeping a flat body position in the water. Finally, children can attempt to glide across and kick with legs unaided.

Progression 4

Once confidence has been developed with the above activities, attention can focus upon back crawl arms. Again, this can be demonstrated and practised by the children by first holding onto the side. This time, one float only is to be used under one arm whilst a child propels themselves through the water using legs and one arm. Different conditions of arm and leg use can be set to provide different challenges.

ACTIVITIES FOR YEARS 3 & 4

Children should learn:
* to choose, use and vary strokes and skills, according to the task and the challenge
* to improve linking movements and actions

SHORT ACTIVITIES

Space Walk

Resources – None

Task – Individually, children cross the pool and imagine they are moving in outer space. They can make large slow steps or they can jump and bound over large craters. Develop activities that encourage children to take their feet off the bottom of the pool.

Relays

Resources – Batons

Task – In pairs or small groups, children race each other across the pool, passing a baton as they go. Such races should however be conditioned to include all abilities. Therefore some could walk, others bound, some use floats and others swim.

Star Float

Resources – None

Task – Children aim to float on the surface whilst making a star shape with spread arms and legs. Children start by leaning backwards in the water, placing their ears in the water and looking at the ceiling. The challenge is to lay completely still for approximately five seconds. If water confidence is sufficiently high, then this can be repeated but modified to be face down.

Pencil Jump

Resources – None

Task – Children jump into the water, from the side with hands above head. They should enter the water straight and bend knees when landing. As children become more confident, they should be encouraged to go into deeper water so that they can jump into and below the surface. Different shapes in the air can also be attempted e.g. tuck jump.

FOCUS ACTIVITIES

Progression 1

Recap working on front crawl starting with legs first. From holding onto the side, to supporting the body whilst swimming with a float under each arm, before moving on to the holding of one float out in front. Activities should always stress keeping a flat body position in the water. Children should also attempt to glide across and kick with legs unaided. Arm practices should be recapped. Attention should then focus again upon front crawl arms. This can be demonstrated and practised by the children by first holding onto the side, before using one float only (to be used under one arm) to propel themselves through the water using legs and one arm. Different conditions of arm and leg use can be set to provide different challenges.

Progression 2

Recap working on back crawl starting with legs first. From holding onto the side, to supporting the body whilst swimming with a float under each arm, before moving on to the holding of one float over the chest. Activities should always stress keeping a flat body position in the water. Children should also attempt to glide across and kick with legs unaided. Attention should then focus again upon back crawl arms. This can be demonstrated and practised by the children by first holding onto the side, before using one float only (to be used under one arm) to propel themselves through the water using legs and one arm. Different conditions of arm and leg use can be set to provide different challenges.

Progression 3

Begin with working on breaststroke, starting with legs first. Initially this can be done by holding onto the side. Children start with their legs straight out behind them ('pencil'). Then bend them up to their bottom ('bend') and then separate them ('star'). Carry this out and consolidate the order. Follow this by supporting the body whilst swimming with a float firstly on back, then on front. Focusing on breaststroke arms, children can model starting with arms stretched out in front. Then making small circles (around a 'bowl') into the chest, before scooping hands forward under the water in a praying position back to the beginning – out in front. Practice of action can then be consolidated by swimming with a woggle under the arms before trying without buoyancy aids. Remember, as the stroke begins to develop, the ratio is one arm pull to one leg kick with the order of pull, breath, kick, glide.

ACTIVITIES FOR YEARS 5 & 6

Children should learn:
- to consolidate and develop the quality of their skills
- to improve linking movements and actions
- to choose, use and vary strokes and skills, according to the task and the challenge

SHORT ACTIVITIES

Fetch!

Resources – Multiple objects

Task – Children collect as many objects as possible that are scattered across the floor of the pool. Objects can vary in shape, weight and size and can be collected individually or in pairs. Conditions can also be set, such as passing through a hoop before it is picked up and returned.

Over We Go

Resources – None

Task – Children begin by pushing and gliding off the wall with their hands above their heads. Next they repeat but pull their arms quickly back to their hips and push their head downwards and complete a rotation.

Straddle Jump

Resources – None

Task – Children start with their non dominant foot on the edge of the pool, before taking a very large step/ lunge into the water. As they lunge they should lean forward, spreading arms and legs. As they enter the water and try and keep the head above the water.

Sculling

Resources – None

Task – To develop their ability to be relaxed floating and moving in water, children should learn how to 'scull'. This they can do by laying back and floating (no leg kicks), before they start to pull water towards them by making small actions by the side of the body.

FOCUS ACTIVITIES

Progression 1

Recap working on front crawl starting with legs first. From holding onto the side, to supporting the body whilst swimming with a float under each arm, before moving on to the holding of one float out in front. Activities should always stress keeping a flat body position in the water. Children should also attempt to glide across and kick with legs unaided. Arm practices should be recapped. Attention should then focus again upon front crawl arms. This can be demonstrated and practised by the children by first holding onto the side, before using one float only (to be used under one arm) to propel themselves through the water using legs and one arm. Different conditions of arm and leg use can be set to provide different challenges.

Progression 2

Recap working on back crawl starting with legs first. From holding onto the side, to supporting the body whilst swimming with a float under each arm, before moving on to the holding of one float over the chest. Activities should always stress keeping a flat body position in the water. Children should also attempt to glide across and kick with legs unaided. Attention should then focus again upon back crawl arms. This can be demonstrated and practised by the children by first holding onto the side, before using one float only (to be used under one arm) to propel themselves through the water using legs and one arm. Different conditions of arm and leg use can be set to provide different challenges.

Progression 3

Recap working on breaststroke, starting with legs first. Initially this can be done by holding onto the side. Children start with their legs straight out behind them ('pencil'). Then bend them up to their bottom ('bend') and then separate them ('star'). Carry this out and consolidate the order. Follow this by supporting the body whilst swimming with a float firstly on back, then on front. Focusing on breaststroke arms, children can model starting with arms stretched out in front. Then making small circles (around a 'bowl') into the chest, before scooping hands forward under the water in a praying position back to the beginning – out in front. Practice of action can then be consolidated by swimming with a woggle under the arms before trying without buoyancy aids. Remember too as the stroke begins to develop, the ratio is one arm pull to one leg kick with the order of pull, breath, kick, glide.

Progression 4

Begin to develop basics of butterfly stroke, starting with dolphin leg kick. Explain to the children that all of the movement comes from the hips and involves making small leg kicks forwards and backwards. Try kicking under the water from a push and glide (using floats if required). Use of arms can be demonstrated making a key hole shape under the water with recovery over the water. This can be practised with a float between the knees if needed. Dolphin leg kick can be added and children should be reminded to keep kicking throughout the stroke.

OUTDOOR & ADVENTUROUS ACTIVITIES (OAA)

Outdoor and Adventurous Activities (OAA) is easily the most neglected area of the PE National Curriculum. The reasons for the neglect are obvious which include a lack of training, a lack of resources and the fact that the present curriculum only requires teaching OAA in Key Stage 2 and now allows schools the opportunity to drop it altogether if they so wish. In a number of schools OAA is still of course apparent but increasingly due to pressure on the timetable, it manifests itself as just an end of Key Stage 2 trip to an activity centre.

Schools, however, have over recent years steadily invested in developing their own outdoor environments not least because of the desire to provide a safe and stimulating area for younger children to engage in outdoor play, important for instance when delivering the physical development strand of the Foundation Stage. Increasingly too, teachers are being encouraged to deliver other strands such as personal, social and emotional development and communication language and literacy through these outdoor activities.

In the interests of continuity and progression the seemingly obvious idea would be to develop provision of Outdoor and Adventurous Activities into Key Stage 1 which would underpin the programme of study outlined in the PE National Curriculum for Key Stage 2 shown below:

Pupils should be taught to:

a.   take part in outdoor activity challenges, including following trails, in familiar, unfamiliar and changing environments
b.   use a range of orienteering and problem solving skills
c.   work with others to meet the challenges

The lesson ideas provided are linked to the following QCA Schemes of work for Physical Education:

Year 1 & 2:   **(Unit 19) Outdoor and Adventurous Activities 1**

Year 3 & 4:   **(Unit 20) Outdoor and Adventurous Activities 2**

Year 5 & 6:   **(Unit 30) Outdoor and Adventurous Activities 3**

KEY POINTS FOR IMPLEMENTATION

From the teacher's perspective, the key to delivering OAA is the pursuit of being **SECURE**.

Safety – For obvious reasons, Outdoor and Adventurous Activities often carry a larger element of risk than classroom based sessions so it is important that all necessary precautions are taken in preparation e.g. clearing ground and checking equipment. When taking children off site it will also be necessary to carry out a risk assessment (see useful references on page 118).

Engagement – Pitching activities at the right level for a particular class or group can be more difficult than it first appears. Tasks which are too basic quickly become boring and tasks which are too difficult can become frustrating or frightening. The key therefore is to plan sessions which have clear instructions and provide sufficient challenge.

Co-operation – Working with others is central to many of the suggested activities and as such, OAA lends itself readily to learning to work as part of a team and adopting different roles. The encouraging (or engineering) of different groupings always throws up some interesting surprises!

Understanding – Fostering a climate of understanding is vital when considering the strengths and weaknesses of oneself and others. Also in order to co-operate and collaborate fully in a physical environment, children need to develop a level of respect and trust for each other (and their teacher).

Resources – The planning and organisation of practical outdoor sessions can make or break OAA so detailed preparation is vital. Though initially resources for the suggested activities will need to be made or collected, it will be time well spent.

Evaluation – The process in OAA is as important, if not more important than the outcome, so when appropriate, time should always be built in to discuss and reflect upon the lesson. Such key questions may include – What was your role? What did you do in the group? What did others do? What went well? Could you have done anything better? How did you feel when you….?

ACTIVITIES FOR YEARS 1 & 2

Children should learn:
- to recognise their own space
- to explore finding different places
- to follow simple routes and trails, orientating themselves successfully
- to solve simple challenges and problems successfully

Touching Base

Resources – Six large hoops randomly laid out on the ground

Task – Children should find a space and on the command of 'GO', they must find a hoop and touch it, without making contact with anyone else. Once the hoop is touched they must remain in contact with it. Try the activity with fewer hoops for a real challenge!

The Name Game

Resources – One small ball per group, with groups of about ten children

Task – Groups begin in a circle. One child stands in the centre and the ball is rolled or thrown at random around the team, with the child in the centre calling the name of the catcher. The ball has to be returned to the child in the centre each time. Challenges can include making ten consecutive catches or counting how many rolls are completed in one minute.

Keep It Up!

Resources – One ball and one large piece of material per group

Task – Using the material, see how many times a group can make a ball go up in the air. Groups can also be challenged to get the ball through a hoop or over a net.

Alphabet

Resources – None

Task – Divide children into threes and call out the letters of the alphabet at random. Each group must form the shape of the letters called as quickly as possible using their bodies with all group members being used. Larger groups could have the task of making small words.

All Aboard

Resources – Hoops or ropes

Task – On the command of 'All Aboard', children are challenged to get as many of them as possible inside a hoop or a rope circle. Nobody may touch the ground outside the circle and this must be held for a number of seconds.

Rope Trail

Resources – Long rope and varied gym equipment

Task – A variety of gymnastic equipment can be set out in the available space before a long rope is woven around the apparatus. Children are challenged to see if they can follow the path of the rope, under, over and around the objects set out.

Treasure Hunt

Resources – Treasures and writing materials

Task – Children work in pairs. One child from each pair hides objects/treasures and then guides the other child in the pair by giving basic instructions in order to locate objects. Treasure hunts are best started using simple directional commands such as forward, backwards, left and right. Children will also need to know what is meant by a 'pace' or 'step'. Knowledge and understanding of the points of the compass can easily be developed as an extension.

Observation Trail

Resources – Coloured arrows, Question sheets and writing materials

Task – A trail of arrows is marked out around all available space, which can also be completed inside school too. Children are encouraged to spot the next arrow before moving on. Children respond to the question sheet provided as they follow the trail, which could ask such things as 'how many windows have you passed?' or 'how many trees can you see from here?'

Map Making

Resources – Writing materials

Task – Using a basic plan of the classroom, ask children to mark on where they and others sit. Other prominent features can also be added. This can just be graphical at first before moving on to making plan view maps in later years. Try and find challenges that use the maps that have been made, such as place random objects around the room and ask children to locate them on their map.

It's An Order

Resources – None

Task – Ask children if they can arrange themselves in an order. Ideas could include height, alphabetical order of names, birthdays etc.

Gone Fishing

Resources – A variety of equipment

Task – A river is marked out by using ropes or benches. Children must work together and use the equipment provided on the 'bank' such as ropes, hockey sticks or tennis rackets to rescue objects which have been placed in the river. No body parts, including hands, can be placed in the river.

ACTIVITIES FOR YEARS 3 & 4

Children should learn:

- to develop the range and consistency of their skills and work with others to solve challenges
- to choose and apply strategies and skills to meet the requirements of a task or challenge

Hear My Voice

Resources – Blindfolds

Task – Children stand on the far side of a space and put on blindfolds. Everyone walks towards the sound of the teacher's voice. Once the class has started moving the teacher should move around and continue talking.

Farmyard

Resources – None

Task – Children find a space, get down on all fours and close their eyes. Ask each child to choose an animal, either cow, sheep, dog or cat. On the command of 'GO', each child must either moo, baa, woof or miaow. The aim is to move around the space and try to find and meet up with the same animals. By the end, if it has gone well, there should be four groups!

Total 15

Resources – Number cards

Task – In groups of nine, children take a card and number themselves 1 – 9. The children form a circle around number 5 and arrange themselves so that everyone opposite each other, plus the number 5, adds up to a total of 15.

Blindfold Walk

Resources – Blindfolds and various objects to create a basic obstacle course

Task – Children work in pairs. The first leader of the pair guides the blindfolded child safely around an obstacle course using only verbal commands. Swap roles upon completion.

Chasing Your Tail

Resources – None

Task – In groups of at least ten, children should make a chain by placing their hands on the waist of the person in front of them. The person at the front of the line must try and catch the person at the back of their own line. This can be expanded into chasing the tail of another line.

Ups-a-daisy

Resources – None

Task – Children should link hands and arrange the group so that each alternate child has their feet off the floor. The link must not be broken. Additional challenges can be set by asking for feet off the floor for thirty seconds or by supporting another child.

Mushroom Runs

Resources – A large piece of material or a parachute

Task – Children hold the material at regularly spaced intervals and lift it into the air. Children who are then identified by letters, colours of eyes, hair or socks run underneath to the opposite before the material 'mushroom' falls on them.

Switch Around

Resources – One bench per group

Task – All the group stand on their bench and are given a random number. Without leaving the bench they must rearrange themselves in number order. Trying this with upturned benches can be attempted with care.

Crossing The Stream

Resources – Ropes and hoops

Task – A stream is marked out by using ropes. Small groups of children are to use the hoops provided as stepping stones in order to cross the stream. If a child steps out of the hoop the group begins again. Only four feet are allowed in any one hoop at any one time. Take hoops away or allow only three feet in a hoop to make the challenge more difficult.

Loop The Hoop

Resources – Hoops

Task – Organise children into groups of about ten, facing the centre and holding hands. A hoop is looped over one child's arm to start. The hoop must be passed around the circle and must pass over the head of all team members. The task is complete when the hoop is returned to the starting point. Children should not break their grip. More hoops can be added for variation.

Scavenger Hunt

Resources – Coloured markers and/or assorted objects

Task – In a safe, defined space, children are asked to locate same coloured markers or specified objects. This could follow a specific order too and may involve basic maps should it be felt useful.

Wheel Orienteering

Resources – Numbered markers with pictures, cards and writing materials

Task – Randomly, numbered markers are placed around the room to make the largest circle possible in the space available. The teacher stands in the centre to help and observe. Children work in pairs or small groups and are given a control card and set off for their first number. The children visit the markers in the order on their card and draw the picture next to the correct number. The challenges to be completed can be made more complex over time (see end of the unit for sample resources).

ACTIVITIES FOR YEARS 5 & 6

Children should learn:
- to develop and refine orienteering and problem-solving skills when working in groups and on their own
- to decide what approach to use to meet the challenge set
- to adapt their skills and understanding as they move from familiar to unfamiliar environments

SHORT ACTIVITIES

The Zip

Resources – None

Task – Organise children into lines of eight to ten. Each child puts their right hand back through their legs and grips the left hand of the child behind. On the command of 'GO' the person at the back of the line must sit down and the team should pass over them backwards. The first line to finish without breaking their grip stands up.

Human Jumble

Resources – None

Task – Groups of eight to ten children form a circle and place their hands towards the centre. Each child grasps somebody's hand with their right hand and another child's hand with their left hand. The group must work together to untangle the jumble without breaking their grip.

Snakes

Resources – Two long ropes and a selection of cones, hoops and ropes

Task – Divide the children into two groups and spread them evenly along the length of two long ropes, which they should then pick up. Without letting go, switching position or allowing the rope to touch the ground, each group should follow a basic course of manoeuvring around cones or through hoops.

Shape Shifting

Resources – Blindfolds and long ropes

Task – With blindfolds on, each group must form a variety of shapes with the rope, starting with a square. Try a circle for a real challenge!

Little Voice

Resources – One hoop and six random objects per group

Task – In small groups, one group should communicate to another group which objects they should place in their hoop. This must be done without any form of verbal communication. Try this activity over increasingly wide distances.

Out Of Line

Resources – Sixteen coloured bibs or bands (e.g. 4 yellow, 3 blue, 3 red, 3 green, 3 orange)

Task – Each child is given a coloured bib or band. A group must arrange itself in a 4 by 4 grid in which no other child is wearing the same colour in the same row, either vertically, horizontally or diagonally.

Total Transfer

Resources – A variety of equipment

Task – A group must move themselves between one gym mat and another without touching the ground. They should use the equipment provided and they must also take it all with them. A large object like a box or even a cup of water can be transported too just to make the challenge more interesting.

Night Line

Resources - Blindfolds, short ropes and a longer rope

Task - Organise the children into groups of six. Each group is blindfolded and joined together by a rope. By touch alone the children follow a line around a safe, pre-prepared course, with the lead person in each group giving the directions etc. The line can be strung around various points in the school's grounds. Large apparatus can be added to add greater challenge.

Point To Point Orienteering

Resources – Master maps, markers, control cards, record cards

Task – Basic orienteering where children have to visit the markers laid out around a given area in an order that they choose. A group of around four should use their maps to decide on a route. The group should stay together at all times. The markers should then be located and a basic task completed. This can be to record a symbol or number on a card or solve a code. It is important to fix a time when all children should return. Indeed, an example of a timed challenge could be to locate and record as many markers as possible in 20 minutes.

PART THREE

Appendices

OAA RESOURCES

What follows is a number of ready made resources that can be used flexibly to construct different trails and orienteering layouts.

Ensure before such resources are used that a clear map, suitable to the age of the child, is available. Only after this has been devised can the different cards be used and placed at different locations. It is suggested that the 6 x 6 number and letter grids be used with Key Stage 2 and the colour and shape cards used with Key Stage 1.

There is no reason why children should not just record what they find on sheets of paper when they arrive at a checkpoint card but should they require a recording card as they progress, then blanks have also been included. These can be used in many different ways but asking children to identify different letters and numbers using co-ordinates is most effective.

1

A	X	R	N	1	P
W	2	F	6	C	8
Q	Y	J	O	V	G
5	B	10	U	Z	I
L	3	H	S	4	K
9	E	M	7	D	T

2

D	4	O	G	8	J
7	N	9	W	C	U
K	5	F	10	M	R
X	3	S	Z	1	H
Q	A	2	L	Y	V
I	6	T	E	P	B

3

V	H	Z	B	5	E
O	7	K	8	P	2
A	W	6	S	J	M
3	R	F	9	X	D
Y	I	4	N	10	T
G	U	Q	1	C	L

4

L	W	C	3	S	U
10	P	Z	J	N	A
E	4	I	9	V	7
1	Q	8	F	Y	G
K	D	X	5	R	2
O	6	H	T	B	M

5

C	1	H	R	L	X
M	Z	10	Q	2	B
S	J	V	9	F	G
8	7	A	P	3	Y
D	N	4	6	K	T
U	I	W	E	5	O

6

J	R	O	V	B	K
Y	D	5	M	U	4
E	7	H	Z	9	G
S	1	W	L	Q	10
6	A	8	X	3	F
I	T	P	C	2	N

7

D	U	I	E	6	A
1	Q	Y	9	R	2
H	7	M	P	X	J
L	V	O	N	3	F
10	S	4	W	T	8
C	5	G	K	Z	B

8

4	A	H	5	V	O
G	T	K	N	I	6
2	M	8	U	P	W
S	F	Y	L	C	J
B	1	D	Q	X	9
10	R	7	Z	3	E

9

S	B	O	H	L	3
5	W	8	V	9	C
G	N	2	E	6	Y
X	7	J	10	Q	I
A	T	1	R	4	Z
K	P	F	U	D	M

10

Q	U	W	I	4	E
F	5	B	10	J	7
3	V	R	N	X	H
C	8	Y	6	Z	T
9	L	M	G	1	A
P	2	D	S	K	O

1

pink

e

2

orange

c

3

red

g

4

green

f

5   yellow

a

6   white

j

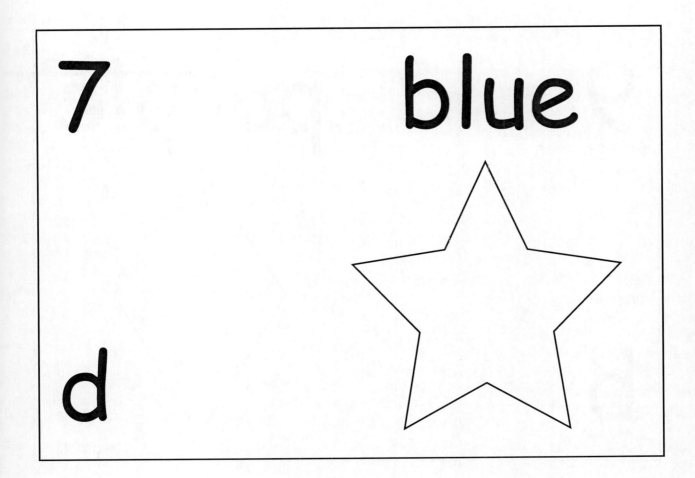

7

blue

d

8

brown

h

9

purple

b

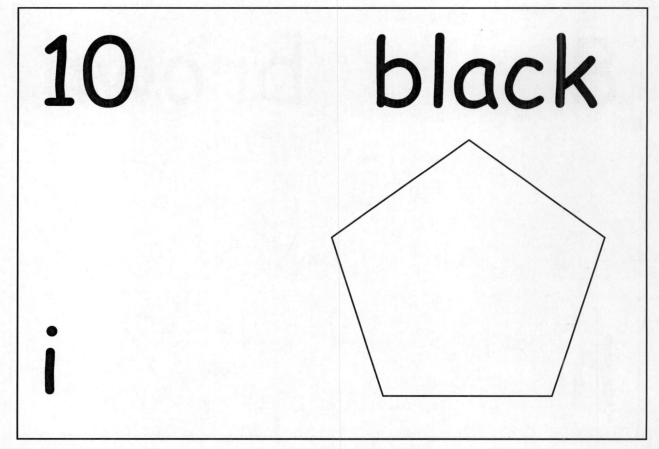

10

black

i

Number	1	2	3	4	5	6	7	8	9	10
Co-ordinates										
Letter										
Word										

Number	1	2	3	4	5	6	7	8	9	10
Co-ordinates										
Letter										
Word										

Number	1	2	3	4	5	6	7	8	9	10
Co-ordinates										
Letter										
Word										

Number	1	2	3	4	5	6	7	8	9	10
Co-ordinates										
Letter										
Word										

ACTIVITY SPECIFIC VOCABULARY

DANCE

- words to describe travel and stillness, e.g. *gallop, skip, jump, hop, bounce, spring, turn, spin, freeze, statue*

- words to describe direction, *e.g. forwards, backwards, sideways*

- words to describe space, *e.g. near, far, in and out, on the spot, own beginning, middle, end*

- words to describe moods and feelings (expressive qualities), *e.g. jolly, stormy*

- words to describe the nature of movement (dynamic qualities), e.g. *fast, strong, gentle*

- words to describe body actions and body parts stimulus (the starting point for dance) words to describe levels, *e.g. high, medium, low*

- words to describe directions, words to describe pathways, *e.g. curved, zigzag*

- words to describe moods, ideas and feelings, *e.g. happy, angry, calm, excited, sad, lonely, tired, hot, sweaty, heart rate warm up, cool down*

- words to describe actions, dynamics, space and relationships, *e.g. bending, stretching, pointing, different rythms and patterns using body sounds such as stamping or clicking fingers*

- words to describe group formations, *e.g. square, circle, line partner, copy, follow, lead*

- gesture words to describe choreographic devices, *e.g. unison, canon, repetition, action and reaction*

GAMES

avoiding	tracking a ball	rolling	striking	overarm
speed	throwing	bouncing	catching	space
rebound	aiming	direction	passing	controlling
shooting	scoring	possession	ball	goal
pass	send	receive	dribble	travel
support	control	rules	tactics	batting
fielding	bowler	wicket	tee	base
boundary	innings	rounder	backstop	score
court	target	net	striking	hitting
defending	attacking	tactics	scoring	shielding
width	depth	marking	covering	positions
stance	crease	batting	pitch	over
innings	forehand	backhand	volley	overhead
rally	singles	doubles	court	win
lose	draw	racket	hoop	cone
serve	competitive	cooperative		

GYMNASTICS

- words to describe speed, *e.g. stop, still, slowly, fast*

- words to describe shape, *e.g. tall, long, wide, narrow, twisted, curled, wide, narrow*

- words to describe direction, *e.g. up, down, forwards, backwards, sideways*

- words to describe level, *e.g. high, low, medium*

- words to describe pathway, *e.g. zigzag, straight, angular*

- words to describe body parts and surfaces, *e.g. feet, hands, toes, heels, knees, head, elbows, bottom, back, tummies, legs, arms, hips, fingers, shoulders, sides, along, around, across, on, off, over, under, through, towards, in front, behind*

jump	land	rock	roll	grip
hang	push	pull	bounce	skip
step	spring	crawl	slide	along
around	across	on	off	over
under	through	towards	in front	behind
tension	extension	relaxation	swing	sequence
copy	upside-down	take off	smooth	quarter-turn
hop	inverted	contrasting	flow	combination
half-turn	sustained	explosive	rotation	spinning
axis	asymmetry	symmetry	matching	flight
crouch	counterbalance	straddle	balance	headstand
handstand	cartwheel			

SWIMMING

walk	hop	skip	run	push
pull	arms	kick	legs	front
back	glide	armbands	floats	support
breathe	underwater	crawl	breaststroke	scull
diving	tuck	streamlined	turning	butterfly
dolphin				

ATHLETICS

run	catch	hop	skip	step
sideways	forwards	backwards	throw	high
low	far	near	straight	aim
drop	bounce	fast	medium	slow
safely	jump	sprint	jog	pace
sling	push	pull	power	stamina
speed	relay	time	measure	record
race	run-up			

OUTDOOR AND ADVENTUROUS ACTIVITIES

listen	explore	plan	maps	diagrams
symbols	trail	seek	find	challenges
problem	solving	scale	orienteering	strategies
review	teamwork	collaborate	roles	controls
responsibilities				

USEFUL REFERENCES

It is always difficult to identify good quality references from which to find out the most appropriate information for teaching PE. Below is a top ten list of places to start which should provide access to all the most current information about the subject and good principles upon which to build.

www.qca.org.uk

The Qualifications and Curriculum Authority website contains a whole range of useful documents, including all the DfES Schemes of Work, High Quality PE and School Sport and advice on issues such as Inclusion and Assessment.

www.teachernet.gov.uk

Teachernet provides information on a range of current issues in education and is also a place where more useful PE documents can be located, such as the Swimming Charter and the Physical Education, School Sport and Club Links (PESSCL) strategy.

www.nc.uk.net

Having access to the National Curriculum online is particularly useful, especially when planning. It is also saves carrying the document around.

www.ncaction.org.uk

An excellent site for assessment purposes, which allows clips to be viewed regarding different activities, different Key Stages and different levels of ability.

www.ofsted.gov.uk

An unlikely recommendation perhaps but the PE subject reviews make fascinating reading and highlight key areas upon which all schools could build.

Safe Practice in Physical Education & School Sport (BAALPE)

Always the most up-to-date and comprehensive publication on safe practice in Physical Education and school sport. It contains guidance on a range of activities plus generic health and safety recommendations, risk assessments guidelines and updates of recent legislative changes.

Safety and Risk in primary school PE (Severs, J.)

Though the above text is a must for any school, this text is very readable and contains a number of practical solutions and good principles specific to Primary school PE.

Coordinating Physical Education Across the Primary School – A Subject Leaders' Handbook (Raymond, C.)

For those with responsibility for the subject leadership pf Physical Education, this is simply a must read text.

Physical Education Matters (Formerly the British Journal of Teaching PE)

An academic journal, published quarterly, which discusses topical issues within PE and contains a pull out section entitled 'Primary PE Focus'.

www.afpe.org.uk

The newly formed Association for PE (afPE) caters for the needs of all within the profession and the site provides links to a multitude of information including opportunities for CPD.